"It is no secret that ministry is tough—in fact, numerous studies show it is one of, if not the most, stressful professional endeavors. Worse, other studies reveal ministers are ill-equipped to face inherent struggles (and some are even taught that struggle is a sign of weakness). This is not biblical. Steve Hall's response is. His unique and holistic approach to a new 'five Ws' is invaluable. No longer should ministerial soul health be deficient or neglected. No longer must astounding numbers of ministers quit or find solace in ungodly solutions. Instead, ministers and leaders now have a solid paradigm that leads toward resiliency and fulfillment of ministry. Minister, you are not alone. And thanks to Steve Hall, you are not without guidance. Read his insights, find strength in community with others, and fulfill your ministry!"

—**Lance M. Bacon**, Discipleship Director,
Lexington Church of God, South Carolina

"There are ministry books which every preacher should read. Certainly, Steve Hall's newest book is one of those. It is, beyond that, a book every churchgoing, church-loving believer should read."

—**Mark Rutland**, President, National Institute of Christian Leadership and Global Servants

"Dr. Steve Hall is a friend and respected colleague. His book *The Uniqueness and Danger of Ministry* is a wonderful treasure trove of resources for nurturing the soul health of ministers and their families. Two things from this book stand out in bold font: first, it is a practical resource that flows from the author's thirty-eight years of experience as a pastor and a pastor to pastors; secondly, he has wisely chosen to focus on preventative, 'upstream' resources, more so than 'after the flood' post-crisis treatment."

—**Gary W. Moon**, Founding Executive Director, Martin Institute and Dallas Willard Center

"It has been said that a pastor's spouse is the loneliest position there is. I would agree. Who do we talk to? Not the church members. Not our colleagues, for fear of sending the message that we are not qualified for our position. Do we talk to our spouse? Often, that answer is no because they are dealing with enough already. This book will teach pastors and spouses how to guard not only their ministry, but also each other and their family."

—**Teresa Holder**, President, Empowered Florida Women

"This book is long overdue. Denominational and local churches often excel at rescuing and restoring ministers who suffer spiritual failure, but so often fail in proactive soul health strategies that prevent burnout and failure. I pray for the wide distribution and implementation of the incredible principles described by Dr. Steve Hall."

—**Lamar Vest**, Former President and CEO, American Bible Society

"Wow! And about time! As one who is listed in the categories of professional minister, pastor's wife, and soul care practitioner, I am elated to read a book that speaks to the heart who cries silently for revelation and restoration. Dr. Steve Hall, along with his wife, LaDon, are true-to-the-core people. I appreciate how they incorporated their multiple years of ministry experience to excellently explain the highs and lows of ministry life and provided suggested solutions."

—**Sharon D. Jones**, Human Resource Pastor, New Hope Church of God, Waldorf, Maryland

"Every career comes with its challenges, but those in everyday ministry know the extra, unique level of 'danger' that comes from following a vocation that involves the pitfalls associated with Kingdom service. Steve Hall looks through the lens of experience and integrity from a lifetime of pastoral leadership to bring a forthright and sincere approach to the all too familiar dangers of full-time Christian ministry."

—**Gary Lewis**, General Overseer, Church of God, Cleveland, Tennessee

"Ministry is holy work. But it is also heavy work. It can bless you one moment and burden you the next. It demands presence, empathy, courage, and spiritual discernment. Yet amid the preaching, planning, praying, and pastoring, we must ask ourselves: How is my soul? Too many ministers serve faithfully while silently suffering. The pace, pressure, and pain of ministry can take a toll on our emotional, mental, and spiritual well-being. And when our soul health deteriorates, everything else begins to suffer. Take good care of your soul and the souls of your family by reading this book."

—**Stan Holder**, Administrative Bishop, Florida Church of God

The Uniqueness and Danger of Ministry

The Uniqueness and Danger of Ministry

A Soul Health Manual for Ministers and Their Families

STEVE HALL

Foreword by Gary Oliver

WIPF & STOCK · Eugene, Oregon

THE UNIQUENESS AND DANGER OF MINISTRY
A Soul Health Manual for Ministers and Their Families

Copyright © 2025 Steve Hall. All rights reserved. Except for brief quotations in critical publications or reviews, no part of this book may be reproduced in any manner without prior written permission from the publisher. Write: Permissions, Wipf and Stock Publishers, 199 W. 8th Ave., Suite 3, Eugene, OR 97401.

Wipf & Stock
An Imprint of Wipf and Stock Publishers
199 W. 8th Ave., Suite 3
Eugene, OR 97401

www.wipfandstock.com

PAPERBACK ISBN: 979-8-3852-5491-0
HARDCOVER ISBN: 979-8-3852-5492-7
EBOOK ISBN: 979-8-3852-5493-4

VERSION NUMBER 11/18/25

Unless otherwise indicated, all Scripture quotations are taken from the Holy Bible, New Living Translation, copyright © 1996, 2004, 2015 by Tyndale House Foundation. Used by permission of Tyndale House Publishers, Carol Stream, Illinois 60188. All rights reserved.

Scripture taken from the New King James Version®. Copyright © 1982 by Thomas Nelson. Used by permission. All rights reserved.

Scripture quotations taken from The Holy Bible, New International Version®, NIV®. Copyright © 1973, 1978, 1984, 2011 by Biblica, Inc. Used with permission of Zondervan. All rights reserved worldwide. www.zondervan.com.

Scripture quotations taken from The ESV® Bible (The Holy Bible, English Standard Version®), © 2001 by Crossway, a publishing ministry of Good News Publishers. Used by permission. All rights reserved.

Scripture taken from THE MESSAGE: The Bible in Contemporary Language. Copyright © 2002 by Eugene H. Peterson. THE MESSAGE Numbered Edition copyright © 2005. All rights reserved.

Thayer's Greek Lexicon, Electronic Database. Copyright © 2002, 2003, 2006, 2011 by Biblesoft, Inc. All rights reserved. Used by permission.

To LaDon, my covenant partner for life, bone of my bone, flesh of my flesh. You're my best friend.

Contents

Foreword by Gary Oliver | ix
Acknowledgments | xi
Introduction: Healthy Minister = Healthy Ministry | xiii

1. The ***Why*** of Ministerial Soul Health | 1
2. The ***What*** of Ministerial Soul Health | 25
3. The ***Work*** of Ministerial Soul Health | 47
4. The ***Wisdom*** of Ministerial Family Soul Health | 93
5. The ***Wrap-Up*** of Ministerial Soul Health: A Complete Soul Transmission | 131

Epilogue | 145
Appendix 1: Resources | 147
Appendix 2: Soul Health Planning Toolkit | 150
Bibliography | 167

Foreword

I LOVE GOOD BOOKS. I've written over twenty books, and at one point, I had well over 2,500 books in my personal library . . . way too many.

After many decades of ministry, including five years of graduate and post-graduate theological training, speaking to over a million men at Promise Keeper events across the country, and speaking on five continents, I've realized that, while reading, writing, speaking, and teaching more can be beneficial and profitable, it's actually not his best for us.

The book that God has led Steve to write is one of the most powerful, practical, and applicable books I've read in many years. God's desire for us is that we are men and women who, over time, "become conformed to the image of His Son" (Rom 8:29)—men and women who choose to actually live, look, listen, love, and sound a little more like Him every single day.

It's OK to keep on doing good stuff . . . but to meaningfully invest time in waiting on him, listening to him, and becoming more like him is what our loving Lord continues to invite us to do.

Steve's encouragement to meaningfully eliminate all negative, cynical, deceptive, and draining people, thought patterns, behaviors, and circumstances from our lives and to intentionally invest time in waiting on him—listening *for* and then *to* Him—being still so we can know (heart knowledge) that he is God—is simple, practical, and truly transformational.

In Eph 3:19, Paul encourages us "to know the love of Christ which surpasses knowledge, that you may be filled to all the fullness of God." In this passage, Paul uses two different Greek words for the word "know." He is urging us to actually know (*epiginosko*—heart knowledge) the love of Christ that surpasses mere (*ginosko*—head) knowledge. This is what God has called Steve to help us better understand.

Foreword

I greatly appreciate Steve's encouragement and exhortation for us to adopt an openness to learning from the best practices of all Christian faith traditions, which, when integrated into an orthodox, compassionate, and morally convictional life, will lead to a truly Christlike way of living.

Remember that God doesn't mind breadth, but his heart is for us to experience depth. There's nothing wrong with aiming for bigger and better, but that doesn't necessarily mean it's his best. Over time, the quality of our walk *with* Him determines the quality of our ministry *for* him.

God has used Steve to deliver a uniquely powerful and practical message, and it is clearly for such a time as this! Over the past several years, we have seen significant challenges, difficulties, and spiritual warfare affecting those God has called to vocational ministry. It is impacting the mental, emotional, relational, and spiritual health of leaders in increasingly significant ways, both individually and within their marriages and families. What God has prompted Steve to share will help ministers build a stronger foundation for who God has called them to be and become and what He has called them to do in every aspect of their lives.

If you are a vocational minister or church member, I want to encourage you to not merely read this book but to invest time in pondering and praying over what you sense God might be wanting to say to you about you—about how much he really loves you, how he is inviting you to experience his sovereign joy and become who he actually designed you to be and become from before the foundation of the world.

And then, actually invest time in the simple, practical, and powerful application of what you hear him saying to you. I know this is one of those rare books that you will want to read more than once and share with others.

Gary J. Oliver, ThM, PhD
Clinical Psychologist,
Professor of Psychology & Practical Theology,
Author, *Hope & Healing for Unhealthy Anger*

Acknowledgments

From Steve and LaDon: To all we've served and served with: Each church person and staff member since our career in professional ministry started in May 1987 in Phoenix, Arizona, has contributed to our holistic development. Thank you for your contribution to our lives.

From LaDon: To Steve, I love you. Thank you for loving me in return. Over the past forty years, we certainly put our vows to the test. Thankfully, you were implementing "Soul Health" into our marriage long before you even really knew about it formally. As a result, your love for God and spiritual leadership of our home has led us masterfully through the vows of "for better or for worse, for richer or poorer, in sickness and in health, till death do us part." I don't know what the future holds, but I know who holds the future, and I stand by my promise of "whither thou goest I will go." Thank you for loving me unconditionally.

From LaDon and Steve: To our precious children, Carlin, Olivia and Elijah, our favorite titles are Mom and Dad. Our favorite career appointment is parenting. Our greatest joy in life is being your mother and father. We are so proud of all three of you. Each of your personalities weaves a colorful tapestry woven with strength, thoughtfulness, and humor into our lives. We are so grateful to God for you.

To Carl and Elva Hart, LaDon's parents: Through LaDon's life as a single and then married person, you have exhibited to us both a model of Christian faithfulness. Thank you both for your personal and professional example. That example has provided a brilliant guiding light for life and ministry.

From LaDon: To my covenant sisters Denise Morris, Debbie Sulcer, Tami Wallace, Lisa Potter, Tammy Simmons, and Udella Walker, thank you for taking the risk to go away with me on that first retreat invitation. None

Acknowledgments

of us knew what to expect. Over the years, I have listened to your wisdom, basked in your prayers, learned from your mentoring, escaped through our laughter, and ripened the fruits of the spirit in my life. We have shared profound life experiences, along with the simplicity of shopping, exchanging recipes, and sharing decorating ideas. Our retreats are a sanctuary in time that has brought much soul healing. I am a better person for having all of you in my life. Thank you for sharing your time but, most importantly, your friendship.

Introduction
Healthy Minister = Healthy Ministry

> CAUTION: This book is written for the professional minister. Lay ministers (volunteers), having never served in a professional ministry role, will not fully understand the content herein. Proceed at your own risk!

No one gets lucky with soul health, especially ministers. Don't treat your soul like a slot machine, putting in more conference or church service coins, pulling the proverbial handle of ministry, hoping to get lucky with soul health.

—Steve Hall

I KNOW OF NO other professional vocation more noble and important than ministry. Therefore, it makes sense that the noblest and most important professional vocation would also be inherently unique and dangerous. In this book, I intend to make the case for professional ministry as the most noble and important vocation, followed by identifying its inherently unique and dangerous realities. Also, in this book, I will share how a minister can safeguard their soul and the souls of their family members against the unique and dangerous challenges of professional ministry. The following chapters are organized as ministerial soul health's *why*, *what*, and *work*. I will also address the *wisdom* of a minister thoughtfully considering their family's soul health, and finally *wrap-up* with an introduction to Spiritual Formation as the most robust soul health gym, so to speak.

Introduction

Surely, my story may not be your story. I'm sure that many ministers won't identify with the pain of professional ministry leadership as I or those cited in this book have. My goal is not to paint all ministers with a broad brush of negative paint. My goal is to normalize the uniqueness and danger of ministry for many ministers who identify with my story, research, and recollections of others' stories. If you don't resonate with the uniqueness and danger of ministry I write about, perhaps I can convince you enough that your fellow minister may not have the same positive experience you have. Hopefully, the content of this book will elicit compassion and care, ultimately saving a hurting minister's calling in life. As you will find herein, the empirical and anecdotal evidence provokes a sense of urgency on behalf of ministerial soul health in this cultural moment.

This urgency is what motivates my wife and me on behalf of ministers and the ministry. Furthermore, the urgency is intensified because this cultural moment seems to be quickly softening up to gospel openness regarding personal renewal, church revival, and global awakening. Liberalness in terms of unorthodox doctrine, un-convictional morality, and an unsustainable you-do-you lifestyle is running out of gas. This vacuous orientation toward human life will leave, at least in the West, humanity open to meeting an ancient, living God who offers authentic, deep, and wide contemporary life meaning in this cultural moment. Therefore, Christian ministers of orthodox doctrine, convictional and clear morality, in addition to an embodied faith, need to be the healthiest souls they can be for the sake of the kingdom of God in this cultural moment. This evangelistic urgency also motivates this book.

In contemporary research, ministers are doing okay, albeit their overall well-being scores are less than those of the people who attend their churches.[1] My hunch is that although you may identify to a greater or lesser degree with the following content, you will recognize the unique and potentially dangerous realities of professional ministry. If you agree with me, three things must happen: we must acknowledge the uniqueness and danger of ministry within our ranks, implement proactive soul health resources and programs, and cultivate a generational mindset focused on prevention rather than recovery.

I hope the thread of preventative ministerial soul health is seen throughout this book. In my experience, denominations and church associations are competent at rescue and restoration but incompetent at

---

1. Jensen, *Relationships of Today's Pastors*, 11.

prevention. The obvious problem with this is that competence in rescue and restoration is reactive and not proactive. Ultimately, this book aims to invite you and Christian ministry organizations to a preventative posture of ministerial soul health. Preventative soul health for the minister and their family anticipates a decrease in the need for rescue and restoration, yet more importantly, to increase ministerial satisfaction early, stimulating a sense of holistic well-being that results in longitudinal ministry satisfaction and resilience. In a nutshell, the idea is to build a minister and their support systems strong and healthy early, rather than addressing a minister's weaknesses and disease later. In other words, the urgent issue is that addressing soul health now is better than addressing soul healing later.

Furthermore, I want to make this point up front: continued support of performance-based leadership and academic training without preventative soul health training will accelerate the burnout of contemporary ministers. To this author, soul health is the most glaring absence in contemporary ministry training, where an undue emphasis is placed on kingdom of the world metrics and tactical training rather than holistic soul health. In his book *Flourishing in Ministry*, researcher Matt Bloom provides a wealth of data (surveying more than twenty thousand ministers), concluding that a lack of preventative and ongoing lifestyle strategy related to soul health is seminal for the escalating incidence of burnout among ministers.[2] The unhelpful ministry culture of fixing it later rather than preventing it now has been my reality. Paul David Tripp addresses this from the perspective of placing more emphasis on tactical training (typically academics) than holistic soul health in his must-read book *Dangerous Calling*.[3]

Albeit narrative does not equate to normative, I don't want my historical ministry reality to be the future reality for the students I'm training. Maybe my story, and many others, has been your story; may it not be theirs.

The professional ministry has been my primary vocation for the last thirty-eight years. I've ministered professionally, bi-vocationally and full-time, on staff in Phoenix, Arizona; Fountain Valley, California; Severn, Maryland; and as lead pastor in Severn, Maryland, and Lake Panasoffkee, Florida. Thirty of those thirty-eight years were spent in one church serving as a staff member and lead pastor. I've experienced the unique and dangerous reality of ministry at various levels, in diverse geographies and demographics.

2. Bloom, *Flourishing in Ministry*, 45.
3. Tripp, *Dangerous Calling*, 25.

Introduction

A few years after launching from my undergraduate ministry training, disoriented by the unique and dangerous demands of professional ministry, I found myself in the office of my lead pastor, confessing through tears a disillusionment with the ministry. This disillusionment was not about Bible lesson prep, program organizing, recruiting and training volunteers, conducting an evangelism outreach, or leading small groups. Oh no, I was well-trained for all that professional activity. However, all the unanticipated, unique, and dangerous realities of ministry were disillusioning me.

I told him how disorienting it was to work where I worshiped. I lamented how every week, multiple days a week, my wife and child go to work with me. How their lives are scrutinized and judged, how my wife's service to the church is an unspoken "two for the price of one" deal. He listened to me bellow about how I no longer read the Bible for personal pleasure but only for professional programs. Exasperated, I pointed out that all of my and my family's friends come from where I work and worship. I went further about how, sometimes, after confiding in my friends about work frustration, those friends I worship with reminded me that they pay my salary and love the lead pastor.

Furthermore, they and the rest of the congregation were ostensibly offended by my expressed frustration. I was frustrated about their pastor and church leadership, who happened to be my employer. I was startled to discover that my friends were my co-worshipers and co-employers. Finally, with a crescendo-like flourish, I pointedly recognized that even he, my pastor, was my employer. Where do I go for pastoral counsel and/or prayer about my mental, marital, financial, or work-related struggles? To which he replied incredulously, "You're struggling?" I burst into tears. Not a very manly thing to do, I suppose, but that's where I was.

He sat back, took a deep breath, and said compassionately, "Son, welcome to ministry. You're not experiencing anything anyone in ministry hasn't or isn't experiencing. You're gonna have to suck it up, Buttercup!"

With that counsel, I did just what he said, embraced the suck, and got back to work. Eighteen months later, on the brink of a mental and ministry meltdown, I moved back to my hometown and entered a master's program for clinical pastoral counseling. Of course, this new venture aimed to serve the church better. However, as the program progressed, it became evident that I was just trying to get the help I needed to survive the unique and dangerous vocation of professional ministry. Serving my church with mental health skills became the cover for me to get the help I needed. How about

Introduction

you? How are you trying to get the help you need under the cover of helping others?

Many years of ministry later, after personal counseling, a master's degree in pastoral counseling, and a doctorate in spiritual formation, I've discovered, along the rocky and circuitous way, the skill set for ministerial soul health I needed. My hunch is that this is indeed the skill set you need. So, yes, professional ministry is indeed unique and dangerous. However, suppose the good that could be done if emerging and existing ministers embrace the content in this book and gleaned from Christian history and contemporary ministerial research and reflection. If you adopt the following theory and practice and intentionally apply it, then your future in ministry can be bright, fruitful, resilient, and joyous.

Don't worry; no one in your current ministry context knows you're reading this book. It's okay to keep reading this book a secret. Cover it with plain brown butcher paper, like a middle school math book. Or better yet, do the digital thing with a privacy screen protector. Take it to the doctor's or counselor's office to read in the waiting room. No one will know what you're reading. However, if you permit yourself, perhaps you'll even give up hiding behind the minister hero persona and become a real person in front of and behind the ministry scenes.

A particular word to my Pentecostal/charismatic colleagues, specious Spirit-filled confidence is thin ministerial ice. You may be one straw of ministerial uniqueness or danger away from falling through the ice, taking your family and church with you. Many Spirit-filled ministers, just like you, have deluded themselves with high-octane charismatic ministry, yet fallen through the ice and drowned.[4] The research is clear: Spirit-filled does not guarantee that your soul will be impervious to the unique and dangerous kryptonite of ministry.[5] Spirit-filled or not, as a professional minister, I would consider the theory that follows and the practices offered.

To be clear: despite all the unique and dangerous realities of professional ministry, bi-vocational or not, Spirit-filled or not, you have been called by the God of the universe to serve as his right-hand person on earth. You are promoting his will on earth as it is in heaven through your ministry skill set. Although all work is sacred, professional ministry stands head and shoulders above all other vocations because this work is of eternal weight.

---

4. Bacon, *Restore Such a One*, 23–41.
5. Bowers, *Portrait and Prospect*, 64–49.

Introduction

To clarify what I mean by eternal weight when it comes to vocations, I will be very disappointed if I get to heaven and have to do taxes, change my tire, take an antacid, or put out the trash. Yes, sacred can be the work of tax preparation, tire repair, gastroenterology, and trash collection when offered to glorify God (1 Cor 10:31).[6] But none of that work is eternally oriented day in and day out. Ministry's focus is every day, every minister, everything, everywhere, eternally oriented. This eternal orientation, as we will see, is both the joy and the bother of professional ministry.

To be clear, I want to entice you with the tales of professional ministry danger and trigger you with its uniqueness to provoke a visceral interest in your soul health. Be sure you can thrive in the context of a ministry career. But it will take the ruthless strangulation of old maladaptive ministry expectations and poor soul hygiene habits before you sense that resurrection feeling. Furthermore, thriving in ministry will also take intentional soul health planning and effort far more strategic than any non-professional minister in your church. No one gets lucky with soul health. Stop gambling.

Come on! Take a deep breath that symbolizes your second wind of ministry. Whether you're flying high or low in ministry right now, every professional minister in any context or season can use the following chapters for the sake of soul health. Because, as Bishop Stan Holder is fond of saying to those ministers he serves, only a healthy minister can have a healthy ministry.[7] The direction of soul health conveyance operates in a one-way manner, from the preacher to the parish. Let's get the horse of ministerial soul health in front of the cart of ministerial work. Saddle up!

> NOTE: I will often address principles repetitively but in a different way. This repetition is strategic for the sake of reinforcement, not redundancy.

---

6. All Bible references are from the New Living Translation unless noted.

7. Paraphrase of a comment Stan Holder made at the Replenish Retreat for Church of God ministers of the DelMarVa-DC region, October 2019.

1

The *Why* of Ministerial Soul Health

My father-in-law served in professional ministry for sixty-two years before finally retiring. Consequently, after that long time in vocational ministry, he has plenty of stories supporting the notion that ministry is a unique and dangerous career. During a pastorate in Pasadena, Texas, he led a Sunday worship service billed as the launch of a new era for the church. Growth in attendance and finance was building, and he wanted to harness the momentum with a strategic community outreach service. After much planning, prayer, and perspiration, he came to the offering segment in the service of a packed-out house.

The plan was to subtly highlight the stewardship moment in the service so that visitors wouldn't feel pressured into giving. Then on to pray and invite the pianist to provide the offertory. He had asked both pianists to select and prepare a piece to share. Having both available and prepared ensured that if one got sick, the other could provide for it. What he could not have anticipated was that one pianist was struggling with playing due to a horrid argument with her husband on the way to church that morning. The other privately stewed because she heard she wasn't asked first.

He resolved his prayer and looked at the pianist, who had experienced an earlier spousal conflict, motioning that it was time for them to share the offertory. The pianist promptly crossed her arms, teared up, and shook her head from side to side, turning away from her pastor. Startled, he quickly looked to the other pianist to share her piece and she also crossed her arms,

The Uniqueness and Danger of Ministry

huffed in obvious offense, shook her head from side to side, and turned away from her pastor. Knowing that the two best-laid plan assassins had murdered the service, disheartened, he strode to the piano as the disoriented ushers looked to him wide-eyed for cues about the best next steps for collecting the offering. When he sat down on the piano bench, he released the ushers and, to heightened attention, commenced to play a piano piece, if it can be called that. For the next few excruciating minutes, my father-in-law, having never taken a piano lesson, proceeded to bang ruthlessly on the piano keys to relieve his frustration and punish the petulant pianists who refused to offer their gifts on that special day.

I'm sure you have many comical stories of a similar tone. However, perhaps another story of a more serious nature will help us identify the **Why** of ministerial soul health more poignantly. Maybe this is similar to your story. I use the word "maybe," but I don't mean it. Because, as we will discover, the research indicates it's a safe bet to wager that the following story is similar to one you could tell yourself.

Dr. Angela Reed writes in the *Review and Expositor Journal*,

> Not too long ago, several ministers gathered at Baylor University's Truett Seminary for a series of sessions on spiritual formation for congregations and their leaders. They were asked to read and write about the topic in advance. The group gathered one afternoon to discuss the minister's role as a spiritual guide for congregational members. A lively discussion ensued; nearly every group member offered insights and stories.
>
> Mason, a seasoned pastor in his thirties, was the only one who remained silent. This silence was surprising because he usually shared freely and openly with the group. When Mason finally spoke, he paused for some time to consider his words. He agreed with the notion of a minister as a spiritual guide, but one aspect of the idea troubled him. After serving as a pastor for about a decade, he could not think of anyone who regularly set aside time and energy to provide him with this same kind of spiritual care. He shared the following thoughts from his journal.
>
> Mason: "What I need the most is a spiritual director for myself. My struggle with finding a spiritual director is: Who in the world has time for me? Other pastors are just as worn out as I am. I have pastor friends in the area, but I struggle to find the time to meet with them because of the demands related to ministry. Recently, I wrote this text message to a pastor friend: 'I only have a few short years that my girls want to run up to me for hugs

The Why of Ministerial Soul Health

and kisses, and tonight I yelled at them for doing it because I was preparing for a deacons' meeting when they did. I suck as a dad. I want that moment back so bad, I need to cry. I am looking at pictures of my sweet little girls on my wall. What if one day my girls hate church and hate God because they took away their daddy, and then they hate their daddy as well because he allowed himself to be taken?'" Mason ended with this final line, "My pastor friend never wrote me back."[1]

Who has the energy to rescue someone else when we're drowning? As we will learn here, and you already know if you're a professional minister, loneliness is an excruciating yet inherent reality for the minister and their family. You're not doing anything wrong because you feel lonely. Yet, failing to effectively manage the natural loneliness of ministry is wrong. Managing ministry loneliness effectively is possible. Soon, I will address this professional loneliness and offer practical ways to manage it effectively.

However, before proceeding, I need to clarify the dynamics of calling to ministry, ensuring that everyone reading this understands what I mean by "professional ministry." A good question to lead with is, are you called to preach or pastor? I know I'm dating myself, but as the character Ricky Ricardo on the old *I Love Lucy* show often said when he sensed the potential for confusion, "Lemme splain!"[2]

Although preaching is an aspect of pastoring, for the pastor, preaching is perhaps one-tenth of the ministry work. On the other hand, for the evangelist, preaching is nine-tenths of the ministry work. Both pastor and preacher are particular calls to professional ministry and should be accompanied by appropriate training and expertise. However, in this book, the focus will be primarily on the professional pastor.

Now, what about the word "professional" used above? Intentionally, I distinguish between lay (non-professional) and credentialed (professional) ministers. I do this only to distinguish vocations. There is no qualitative or sacral difference between the work of a lay or professional person. Furthermore, I don't mean to secularize the calling to ministry using "professional," but I only want to distinguish between volunteer and professional ministry roles.

Undoubtedly, all Christians are called to serve in lay ministry, but not all are called to professional ministry. The prophet Jeremiah seems to

---

1. Reed, *Rooted in Relationship*, 303–14.
2. Daniels, *I Love Lucy*.

forecast the unique role of the professional shepherd/pastor when he cites God himself, "And I will give you shepherds according to My heart, who will feed you with knowledge and understanding" (Jer 3:15 NKJV).

The Gospel writer Luke recognizes a Spirit-appointed and anointed leadership structure among the people of God. "Therefore, take heed to yourselves and all the flock, among which the Holy Spirit has made you overseers, to shepherd the church of God, which He purchased with His own blood" (Acts 20:28 NKJV). Furthermore, in Hebrews, the long history of the Spirit providing leaders of God who are set apart from the people of God continues. "Obey your leaders and submit to them, for they are keeping watch over your souls as those who will have to give an account. Let them do this with joy and not with groaning, for that would be of no advantage to you" (Heb 13:17 ESV).

To emphasize the importance of the pastoral leadership role of shepherding supervision, Paul emphasizes in his pastoral mentoring to Timothy that those who spiritually rule well are worthy of double honor, "especially those who labor in the word and doctrine" (1 Tim 5:17 NIV). That said, it's my belief and experience that professional ministry comes with a different burden that is unique and dangerous for the professional minister, spouse, and family on both a heavenly and earthly level.

A biblical example comes to mind from the end of 2 Cor 11. Here, Paul pushes back on his detractors with a cascade of pastoring uniquenesses and dangers. Then, in a climaxing literary flourish, he recognizes that all the earthly demands of professional pastoral ministry he just listed are nothing compared to the heavenly burden for the church a pastor carries daily. Biblical exegete David Garland cites this as a contrast between external and internal pastoral demands in his commentary on 2 Corinthians. The point is "that only a divinely called pastoral professional," albeit often bi-vocational, knows the ministry's external and internal burden.[3] And make that doubly true for the ministry spouse who is always the plus-one in the "two for the price of one" typical ministry hiring deal.

Yes, every Christian is a minister (1 Pet 2:9–10), called to serve the ministry of our Good Shepherd as part of the flock. However, the New Testament takes for granted that only a few are called to sub-shepherd responsibility (see Paul's pastoral epistles for an expansive biblical treatment of this distinction).

---

3. Garland, *New American Commentary*, loc. 12566.

The Why of Ministerial Soul Health

To the professional minister, I'm merely preaching to the choir. However, although any minister reading this will readily identify with how Paul and I describe the profession, very few will know how to mitigate the impact of the ministry's unique and dangerous realities. Yet, back in the eighties, when I responded to my special call to professional ministry, Henri Nouwen declared that every minister's foremost "task is to care of the inward fire so that it can offer warmth and light to lost travelers when needed."[4] I've never forgotten those words, although I largely ignored them the first two decades of my ministry career. How about you? Are you largely ignoring the inward fire of your soul, assuming that because you're a credentialed minister and organize your whole life around the church, discipleship programs, and worship services, your soul is automatically healthy? You know intuitively the news I have for you in the following pages. An indisputable pattern of ministerial soul neglect appears in the here and now and the longitudinal research as a vocational epidemic. Ministers can't depend on getting lucky with soul health.

Listen to Paul David Tripp recount the confession of a top-tier young minister with thousands of members, quality staff, plenty of money, beautiful buildings, and all the tech we often dream of. To the shock of his staff and church leadership, the Monday after Sunday, when he preached a top-notch sermon and affably interacted with the church, he stumbled into a staff meeting with this declaration: "I'm done, I can't do this anymore. I can't deal with the pressures of ministry. I can't face preaching another sermon. I can't deal with another meeting. If I am honest, I just want to leave. I want to leave the ministry, I want to leave this area, and I want to leave my wife. No, there's been no affair. I'm just tired of pretending that I'm someone that I'm not. I'm tired of acting like I'm okay when I'm not. I'm tired of pretending my marriage is good when it is the polar opposite of good. I can't preach this coming Sunday, and I have to get away alone or I'm going to explode. I'm sorry to lay this on you this way, but I'm done—I can't go on."

Tripp follows with this: "For me, the attention-getting thing about this sad scenario, which I've heard way too many times, was not its stunning suddenness but the shocking reality that the pastor lived in this day-by-day ministry community fundamentally unknown and uncared for."[5]

I needed to know. This minister needed to know. You need to know. Your spouse needs to know. Your kids need to know. What do we all need

---

4. Nouwen, *Way of the Heart*, 55.
5. Tripp, *Dangerous Calling*, 31.

The Uniqueness and Danger of Ministry

to know? That we're not crazy or alone. Goodness! Let's take action to preventively intervene on behalf of ministerial soul health and let ministers know they're not crazy or alone. Every minister needs to be reminded that professional ministry is genuinely unique and dangerous and that this reality is normal.

While traveling and speaking to many different groups on ministerial soul health, I've discovered that contrary to the common perception of lay people or professional ministers, soul health is not a given among the ranks of professional ministers.

When I first launched from Bible college into professional ministry, I felt like Tom Hanks looked when he played Mr. Rogers in the major motion picture, enthusiastically hopeful that I would change the world with my dedication to and skill in pastoral ministry. An appropriate moniker for me in my first year of ministry would have been "Pastor Rogers." I felt on the inside how Mr. Rogers looked on the outside, confident and serene. However, fifteen years later, an appropriate new moniker would have been "Pastor Rager," as I felt on the inside more like Tom Hanks looked on the outside in *Castaway* screaming at a volleyball. Both movies offer insight into the uniqueness and danger of ministry.

Even in year fifteen, when the minister still dresses like Mr. Rogers, albeit in the latest preacher fashion style, they often feel like a castaway on the inside, regardless of how they look on the outside. Ministers are experts at appearance management.

Consider the reality of our ministry challenge in this cultural moment. This generation of ministers is the first generation to solve for the internet. I know that I used math language in that last sentence. If you're anything like me with math trauma in your past, the language of math may be a post-traumatic trigger. So, pause here, take a Xanax, or do some deep breathing if you need to; no judgment. Math triggering aside, the formulaic language works here.

Remember, in high school math, the teacher often said, "You will be solving for x, or y, etc., in this problem." Each generation of ministers will have a problem or problems to solve that are unique to them. The problems are cultural variables. These unique problems or variables are the x or y in the current cultural equation. In our current cultural equation, the postmodern one, we face the problem of the digital age. In other words, in this cultural moment, we are solving for the internet variable of ministry in the twenty-first century. For the first time in history, you minister to digital natives who don't know a world without smartphones and the internet at their beck and call. Why do they need God or you? They have the lord ChatGPT. How do you know I'm not using AI right now to write this book, or are you using it to build your sermon for Sunday? It's a wild, wild digital world out there begging ministers to rise like the sons of Issachar and discern the times. What pressure!

Throw in a pandemic and the current fulfillment of Lesslie Newbigin's 1970s concern about politics becoming the new millennium's most influential religion, and you've got a perfect storm for ministers burning down and out of professional ministry.[6] During the pandemic, I did several virtual coping workshops for ministers dealing with the stress of this cultural moment. The overwhelming cry of my soul and those professional ministers I ministered to was the impossible place our current double-bind ministry culture places us in.

In those workshops, ministers echoed my reality, where every sermon was dissected for political correctness on the left and right of the congregation. If a minister addressed issues of race, sexuality, public policy, economics, media, etc., it was a lose-lose eventuality as congregants on one side or another of an issue simply couldn't be satisfied. As the adage goes, if I heard it once, I heard it a thousand times from the lips of honest, faithful, loving, diligent ministers: "Every Sunday, I'm damned if I preach this, or I'm damned if I preach that. I think I'd rather not preach at all." No wonder current surveys reveal a dismal state of ministerial well-being.

A Barna report in April of 2022 notes a sharp increase in the number of ministers considering leaving ministry as a profession, up thirteen percentage points from 29 to 42 percent.[7] This Barna revelation confirms previous research indicating that twenty-first-century ministers are in big trouble regarding holistic well-being.[8]

After experiencing this double-bind era of ministry and hearing so many reports of ministerial despair, finally my mental health antenna went up, and I realized I was experiencing, subjectively and objectively, a form of PTSD, Post-Traumatic Stress Disorder. I later refined this vocational diagnosis to PTSP, Post-Traumatic Stress Pastoring. The following section will underscore the *Why* of ministerial soul health, with particular emphasis

---

6. Newbigin, *Foolishness to the Greeks*, 115.
7. Barna Group, "Pastors Share Top Reasons."
8. Clarke, "Role-Related Stress."

on the uniqueness of ministry and the intrinsic dangers that come with the territory of professional ministry.

PTSP: Post-Traumatic Stress Pastoring

In your pastorate, have you ever experienced the shock and trauma of being blindsided by parishioners who were covertly undermining the very ministry they were overtly supporting? In other words, have you ever been stabbed in the back by the same person or people you've dedicated your life to serving? After discovering this betrayal and other similar events, did the cumulative traumatic experiences induce fear and helplessness? Did you begin to isolate yourself emotionally and avoid relational connections with church folks? Did you become emotionally numb and persistently hyper-vigilant to prevent recurrent negative feelings? Has your sleep, concentration, eating, or mood been affected? Finally, upon hearing about this traumatic experience, did your spouse develop similar vicarious symptoms immediately or eventually?

I've experienced this firsthand and heard many pastors recount attacks from the very people they've sacrificed for and dedicated their lives to serve and bless—like Pastor Dan, who trusted a seemingly spiritual and supportive elder in the church. However, after several years of supporting the elder and personally opening himself to him, Pastor Dan discovered the elder was sowing dissension secretly among church leadership and building support for launching his church. How about Pastor Alex and his wife, befriended by a church couple in leadership? Over time, Alex and his wife came to believe that this couple were more than just typical parishioners; they were true friends whose relationship transcended the usual pastor/parishioner type. However, in one single moment during a church leadership meeting, the couple turned on Alex, exposing privately confessed struggles and raising suspicions of fiscal maleficence. In the ensuing months, the couple successfully split the church and took over half the congregation to their new worship place.

Suppose this describes some traumatic encounters you've experienced throughout your pastoral career. In that case, the *Diagnostic and Statistical Manual for Mental Disorders* indicates you satisfy the clinical diagnosis criteria for Post-Traumatic Stress Disorder (PTSD)[9]. Surprised? I'm not. During thirty-eight years of ministry, I've experienced dozens of these

---

9. American Psychiatric Association, *Diagnostic and Statistical Manual*, 424.

The Why of Ministerial Soul Health

traumatic encounters and listened to many pastoral colleagues describe similar traumas and the resulting symptoms. In a recent pastor's small group setting, I witnessed the accumulation of personal and collegial ministry trauma reach a critical mass. While the connection may seem extreme, as a psychotherapist and pastor, it dawned on me that ministry, like guerrilla warfare in actual war, can result in something similar to clinical PTSD, i.e., Post-Traumatic Stress Pastoring (PTSP).[10] As in guerrilla warfare, you can't protect yourself if you can't discern the enemy. The invisible but increasing stress and personal toll of ministry often lead to deep discouragement, diminishing vocational satisfaction, and moral failure.[11]

These all-too-familiar traumatic experiences, resulting in the build-up of toxic stress over time, debilitate ministers with symptoms similar to clinical PTSD, yet it's better termed PTSP. Many pastors and ministry spouses reported to me suffering symptoms from PTSP, such as losing sleep by reliving the traumatic encounters in dreams or waking up panicked in the middle of the night with a genuine sense that it will happen again. By the same self-report, pastors believe they could suffer a ministry mugging on any Sunday, threatening their career and fiscal security. "Walking on eggshells," "gun-shy," and "hyper-vigilant" are how many pastors commonly characterize their ministry.

I am not suggesting that churches are filled with psychopathic Christians bent on destroying the pastor's health and well-being. I am suggesting, however, that churches are full of what Marshall Shelley calls "well-intentioned dragons," who consistently cause a unique type of vocational trauma.[12] Furthermore, Sam Chand, in his excellent book *Leadership Pain*, makes this statement: "I know one thing about your church. I may have never set foot on your campus, but this one thing I know: at least 10 percent of your congregation are devils."[13] To which all ministers respond, "Duh!"

Compounding this unique ministry trauma is the reality that pastors are frequently first responders regarding emotionally jolting events in the lives of their parishioners, even those who are devils. These events include death, emergency room visits, phone calls from hysterical spouses after discovering an affair, stillbirths, miscarriages, house fires, arrests, domestic abuse, etc. Every frantic phone call is personal to the pastor. No wonder pastors eventually

---

10. Alloy, *Abnormal Psychology*, 159.
11. Muse, "Intensive Out-Patient Therapy."
12. Shelley, *Well-Intentioned Dragons*, 12.
13. Chand, *Leadership Pain*, 33.

The Uniqueness and Danger of Ministry

exhibit symptoms of clinical PTSD, as in cued panic when the phone rings at unusual times or when they see a teary-eyed parishioner approaching quickly from across the sanctuary. Mental health clinicians call these events internal and external cues of trauma response. Could the unusual call or the fast-approaching parishioner mean another death, injury, or tragedy in the pastor's beloved flock, which they shepherd?

There is no psychological or emotional distance for the pastor from those they respond to; it's always personal, unlike the community service first responders. For example, when called to the scene of a suicide, what police officer expects to find a person to whom they're relationally connected? And then have to comfort the family? And then help the family plan for the funeral? And then officiate the funeral? And then follow up months later with prayer and counsel and help sort through the after-death details? And do this for multiple families at a time without end, year after year? No classic first responder, like a police officer or firefighter, experiences the depth of sustained personal loss and responsibility that a pastor does.

A career-long accumulation of what some psychologists term secondary or vicarious stress depletes a pastor's resilience and makes him more susceptible to PTSD-like symptoms.[14] Moreover, pastors have little or no training in mitigating the effects of secondary stress as counselors, police, and firefighters do, exacerbating the problem and often resulting in compassion fatigue.[15] For example, I've never talked to a pastor who said they took a seminary course in self-care related to first responder trauma, let alone the trauma experienced at the hands of devilish parishioners while engaged in ministry. In contrast, first responders like police or firefighters naturally gain psychological and emotional distance because those they respond to are personally unrelated. But, again, for the pastor, it's all personal and a perpetual trauma intrinsic to professional ministry. Imagine an electric piano sustain pedal that is stuck, blaring one sustained traumatic note of collective pain. This illustration may seem dramatic, but my counseling of ministers and professional research provide the evidence and experience that this characterization is all too common.

Finally, the lack of margin may be the straw with the most significant potential to break the pastor's back. I consider it the carbon monoxide of ministry: colorless, odorless, yet deadly. Harken back to my story in the introduction. The pastor is always a pastor, whether in the pulpit, on a plane,

---

14. Benuto, "Secondary Traumatic Stress."
15. Gerander, "Compassion Fatigue."

The Why of Ministerial Soul Health

or on the playground. This vocational uniqueness is equally true for the pastor's spouse.

Furthermore, a pastor's financial, work, social, sports, spiritual, and family life is enmeshed with the church. Most people don't get all their friends or softball teammates from their workplace, or live with the stress that where and how they worship may affect their income and family security, which is unconsciously unbearable for the pastor and his family.[16] Every pastor and their family are on 24/7, no matter what. Only pastors and politicians bear this kind of vocational burden. Yet, politicians do not carry the pastor's eternal burden regarding their work.

Consider these contrasting graphics illustrating the margin between ministry and non-ministry life.

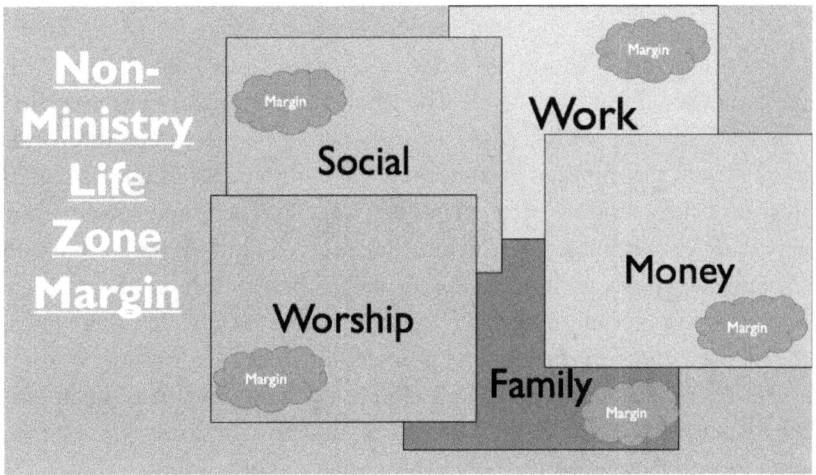

Everyone has standard life zones with limited overlap. A non-ministry life zone margin is intrinsically present in a non-ministry professional's life. For instance, you can easily see, and likely intuit yourself, that a non-ministry professional's worship life and work life don't overlap much. Furthermore, it's unlikely that a non-ministry professional's work and family life overlap much, except for company picnics, etc. However, this is not the case with the ministry professional.

---

16. Visker, "Ministry-Related Burnout."

The Uniqueness and Danger of Ministry

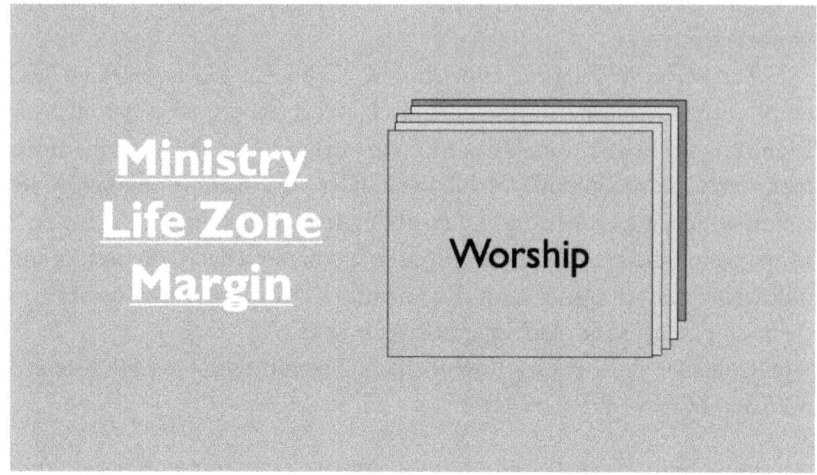

As a ministry family, everyone is deeply invested, like it or not, in the professional minister's work. The whole family worships at the church where the minister works. Multiple times per week, the entire family goes to work with the minister. Furthermore, the minister gets, in full or in part, their monetary support from where they worship. The minister and family gain their most significant social interactions, including friends from where the minister works, worships, and gets paid. Those with whom the ministry family engages socially contribute to the minister's income. In other words, the minister and, by proxy, the minister's family work for those they worship with. What other vocation has this kind of extensive overlap and enmeshment? Beware, the toxic marginlessness of ministry can slowly suffocate the minister and family. Ministry is indeed unique and dangerous.

This lack of margin is due to no fault of the minister or church; it is an inherent uniqueness to ministry. Imagining that the minister is immature or incompetent, resulting in the lack of a life zone margin, would be an incorrect assumption. However, the minister can mitigate the marginlessness of ministry by slowly correcting church culture norms to create more margin in the ministry family life, something I will address in more detail later in the **Work** chapter of ministerial soul health. But for now, let's allow the marginlessness of ministry to lead us into a more profound sense of the **Why** of soul health for ministers.

Pause: Remember, the goal of this chapter is to normalize the inherent uniqueness and danger of professional ministry for any minister of a small

The Why of Ministerial Soul Health

or large church. The bottom line insight I hope you're sensing is that you're not alone or crazy.

Now, back to the *Why* of ministerial soul health. This intrinsic lack of life zone margin creates another opportunity for the symptoms of PTSP to compound in the pastor's mind and heart, leading to compassion fatigue, burnout, or worse. In 2017, the *Clergy Burnout Inventory* found that 65 percent of clergy surveyed bordered on burnout or were in full burnout mode. Typical responses from the survey follow: "I feel used up and spent," and "My family and I feel fatigued and discouraged in ministry."[17] PTSP is real.

Dr. Richard DeShon, a leading expert on job analysis, has studied many professional jobs. When he finished analyzing the job of a local church pastor, he concluded that "the breadth of tasks performed by local church pastors, coupled with the rapid switching between task clusters and roles in this position, is unique. I have never encountered such a fast-paced job with varied and impactful responsibilities."[18]

Laughing through a baby dedication, weeping through a sermon, celebrating healing at the altar, grieving with a family as they pull the plug on a loved one, thrilled about a sizeable financial gift in the morning offering, rocked by receiving a call from a devastated wife after discovering infidelity on the part of their influential church-leading husband, joyfully learning of a young couple's engagement, and, finally, receiving an email from a friend who has decided to leave the church. All in one Sunday.

Professional ministry's uniqueness can be rightly characterized as rife with extreme soul swings for the professional minister. No other vocation has this unique feature related to extremes of human experience. In addition to the uniqueness of soul swings, there is the weight of eternal consequences; it is soul-draining. Can I get a witness?

As one final example of the need for ministerial soul health, I would like to illustrate the trend in mental health within a specific denomination, my denomination, the Church of God, Cleveland, Tennessee. Dr. Tim Maness, the current (2025) Director of Ministerial Care for the Church of God, shared his data on the rise of mental health interest among COG ministers. The center only addresses the mental health concerns of credentialed professional ministers, their spouses, and their families in the Church of God. The following graph is the current trend of ministers accessing mental health support through the COG Ministerial Care service.

17. Visker, "Ministry-Related Burnout."
18. Bloom, *Flourishing in Ministry*, 10.

The Uniqueness and Danger of Ministry

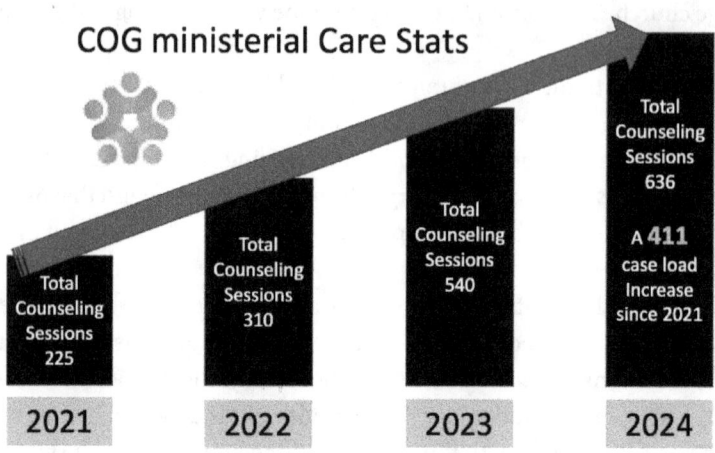

No doubt this is data from within a pandemic. However, Dr. Maness explains that while there is a moderate spike correlated with COVID-19, the trend was ramping up before March 2020.[19] With this graph, it's easy to see how the need for mental health care is increasing yearly among ministers. The trend is not going in a positive direction. But what's the answer? Perhaps ministers just need to suck it up, Buttercups. Or, possibly, there are other more positive ways to turn the trend curve.

Turning the above trend curve individually and corporately demands that we face the harsh and often unconscious sin of embracing ministry metrics of the kingdom of the world as if they are kingdom of God metrics. In other words, repenting of measuring our personal and ministry worth by the ABC metrics of modern ministry: Attendance, Buildings, and Cash. This performance-based, worldly ministry metric is crushing to a minister's soul. How so?

I'm sure that at least every Protestant evangelical[20] minister will be familiar with the typical *Outreach Magazine* cover, measuring the 100 largest and fastest growing churches in America. My point in highlighting these covers is not to criticize *Outreach Magazine* but to underscore

---

19. Tim Maness, private conversation with Director of Church of God Ministerial Care.

20. To be clear, when I use the descriptive term "evangelical," I don't have any political application in mind. I simply mean a Christian orientation that is gospel-centric, orthodox in doctrine, and morally convictional.

the importance of the ABC metrics in modern ministry for this influential periodical's audience. That audience is you and me!

Once again, let me emphasize that I'm not denigrating *Outreach Magazine* for their astute assessment of market demand and then supplying the demand. It's the capitalistic culture water we swim in. The magazine is only accommodating the supply and demand appetite of our contemporary ministry profession.

What came first, the proverbial chicken or the egg? *Outreach Magazine* or a ministerium demanding celebration and sycophantic worship of anything bigger and faster?

In a capitalistic economy with consumerism as its engine, it's only natural for a bigger, faster, richer-is-better mentality to become the standard measure of success. The air we breathe is capitalistic. Westerners are born consumers with success measured by market share. Whereas I believe that capitalism is the best economic system on earth, and I would never want to live in a country that embraces anything different, it is not the economic system of the kingdom of God. Reference God's rationale for selecting David as king, how the early church in the book of Acts sold everything for the common good of all, or how Jesus urged us to seek servanthood to measure success in his kingdom. The kingdom of God metric contrasts, or perhaps a better word would be clashes, with the metric of the world's kingdom.

This line of reasoning begs the question, what's your success metric for ministry? Do you think you're a success because you have a big church, or are you a failure because you don't? Are you successful because you've been invited to the latest ministry conference circuit as a speaker, or do you think you're a failure because you haven't? Come on, you know how your church culture keeps score. The minister with the best ABC stats (translation: bigger or more popular) is intuitively understood as successful, and the minister with the worst ABC stats (translation: smaller or less popular) is intuitively understood as unsuccessful, despite how nice or healthy they are.

Consider Pastor Mike Burnette's confession, ironically, in *Outreach Magazine* itself. In 2018, Pastor Burnette and Life Point Church in Clarksville, Tennessee, were named the Number One Fastest Growing Church in America by *Outreach*. The following year, they were named number seventy-seven. Mike goes on record in *Outreach Magazine* in 2021 about the rise and fall of Life Point:

> When we started getting notoriety for growth, I guess I started believing some of the press about myself. And then I felt that sense

of pressure to stay at the top of the list. I mean, where do you go from No. 1? But the year after we were No. 1, we dropped to No. 77. To be 77 on the church growth list is still great. But it felt like a loss. I remember sitting privately in my office and going, What happened? That was a constant question I asked myself, which is not healthy. I realized I had the wrong goalposts. Truth, I haven't been called to grow a big church; I've been called to lead a church to be healthy.[21]

Can you feel it as you read Mike's struggle with the kingdom of the world metrics? Do you feel the pressure of ministry success based on worldly metrics in your context? Have you ever been to a conference and wondered privately to God why you haven't been blessed with the success of the minister speaking from the stage? Have you ever looked at your denominational ranking of churches and felt a sense of happiness or sadness based on where your church ranked? What minister hasn't felt the heights of joy with Easter attendance only to feel the depths of despair with the abysmal attendance the week after Easter? Mike felt this when his church plummeted from number one to seventy-seven. Performance-based ministry metrics will crush your soul and the soul of your spouse.

After taking a chance on a young pastor and pouring into them and their family as a full-time staff member for a decade, the couple announced that they were heartily disappointed that the church hadn't grown as they anticipated under my leadership. By now, they imagined the church would be much larger and more influential. Furthermore, they were joining a church planter training program and intended to leave my employment to try their hand at pastoring themselves. I affirmed their ministry ambition and ultimately sent them off with a large sum of money to support them. A few years later, the church plant died.

I had a long-term church member tell me they were leaving my church for a church on the other side of town. When I asked why, they sheepishly, with compassion, said, "We just want to be a part of a winning team." Translation: the church across town was growing faster than mine. In the mind of that Christian, I was losing; that other pastor was winning. The following Sunday, a new family showed up at the church I pastored. In conversation, I discovered that they left a smaller church nearby to attend our church, which, in their words, was "outperforming" the church they left. One week later, I was the winning pastor, and another pastor was the

21. Hanewinckel, "Mike Burnette," 141.

The Why of Ministerial Soul Health

losing pastor. This intrinsic performance-based metric steeped in "comparisonitis" in the Western ministry context is another symptom of **Why** ministerial soul health is so critical. I love how Pastor Travis Hall puts it in his podcast episode "The Quickest Way to Lose Yourself Is to Compare Yourself." He speaks of the "con of comparison."[22] So good.

Listen to how Pete Portal, in his excellent book *How to Be (Un)Successful: An Unlikely Guide to Human Flourishing*, expresses the insidious consequences of comparisonitis: "Far from freeing me from my broken sense of self, the version of faith I was trying to live by was exacerbating the core wound I recognized in myself. That wound was a sense of feeling a failure, unsuccessful. And like an unwelcome parasite, it fed on comparison to others."[23]

I, and many ministers I speak to, struggle with the question, "Am I enough?" This question is painfully acute when the church is struggling with attendance and money. Remember, the devil never comes to you with a stick but with an idea, just an idea. The idea typically follows this line of reasoning. The idea that comes to the minister from seemingly nowhere is: I know I'm called, but why are things so hard? What's wrong with me? Why doesn't God bless my church like he seems to be blessing that church? Am I enough? Is he more pleased with them than he is with me? Maybe I don't pray, fast, meditate, read, study, give, serve, love enough. The cascade of devilish ideas is never-ending. Why don't I seem to be enough to earn God's favor for church growth? This typical negative self-feedback loop is nothing new. The ancient monastics in the fourth and fifth centuries described demonic attacks using the weapon of negative self-deprecating ideas.[24]

This ancient evil tactic of creating an accusing flow of ideas is a strong rip current of lies. You can't go with it, and you can't go against it; you've got to lean into God's alternative ideas until you cut across the doubting current enough to get free. You'll need to recite the following Spirit ideas until you can soul-swim out of the rip.

> Since this is the kind of life we have chosen, the life of the Spirit, let us make sure that we do not just hold it as an idea in our heads or a sentiment in our hearts, but work out its implications in every detail of our lives. That means we will not compare ourselves with each other as if one of us were better and another worse. We have

---

22. Hall, *Transformational Truths*.
23. Portal, *How to Be (Un)Successful*, 20.
24. Buxton, *Wisdom of the Desert*, 24.

The Uniqueness and Danger of Ministry

far more interesting things to do with our lives. Each of us is an original. (Gal 5:25–26 MSG)

YOU ARE ENOUGH!

And may you have the power to understand, as all God's people should, how wide, how long, how high, and how deep his love is for you. (Eph 3:18)

YOU ARE ENOUGH!

Our metrics must morph from kingdom of the world metrics to kingdom of God metrics. We must stop trying to earn our keep in the kingdom!

YOU ARE ENOUGH!

Let's pause for a theology break. What is your theology of church growth? Is it possible that God has designed and called you to a small church, a medium church, or a large church? Can a church be big and healthy while a small church is unhealthy? What is your theology of success and can you live with it? Consider this fundamental evangelical summary of church growth theology that I suspect every minister or member reading this book will agree with: Only the Spirit calls, convicts, converts, and conveys souls into the church.

My hunch is that you believe this. My hunch is also that you struggle to live with this. What I mean by living with this is being content with the size of your church but not its health. Yes, relax about church growth. Take a dose of your own church growth theology above, and use it as the antidote for comparisonitis. Or what about the dreaded "if I can only just" syndrome? You know the syndrome, if I can only just break the 125 barrier. If I can only just hire this part-time staff person. If I can only just reach this level of financial giving. If I can only just_____. Your church growth theology can set you free from the crushing cycle of chasing church growth. Of course, strive to excel in all you do. The King of kings deserves only the best. Beyond that, relax into his calling and let him do only what he can do: call, convict, convert, and convey.

Listen to Portal drive the need for a theology of success one more time before we move on:

> What is the effect of the kingdom of God on us? It is "to align our loves and longings with his—to want what God wants, to desire

what God desires, to hunger and thirst after God and crave a world where he is all in all." This different perspective for looking at the world recognizes that who you are is primary to what you do, which in turn leads to a repentance that is less about being sorry for things you have done wrong and more about being sorry you are the kind of person who would do such things. In this way, the kingdom invites us into a life of deepening instinctive internal virtue rather than surface-level rule-following. It is often slow, sometimes painful, always liberating, and promises to make us thoroughly (un)successful. You could define success as correctly directing your love and energy to what is primary and of most importance. While it's easy to become "captivated by rival visions of flourishing" that much of today's culture tries to sell us, "God has created us for himself and our hearts are designed to find their end in him." And yet despite professing faith in Jesus, many of us still spend our days craving rival gods, frenetically pursuing rival kingdoms. This is because there is no reorienting of our true selves and our longings without resistance from our shadow selves: "It is crucial for us to recognize that our ultimate loves, longings, desires, and cravings are learned." I hope that the following chapters will assist you in (un)learning the disordered desires of the world, to make you more successful in living the life God has for you.[25]

YOU ARE ENOUGH!

I really wanted to curse there to punctuate the point dramatically! A curse word just feels right. What curse word would you use after "enough"? Remember, it's not a sin to be tempted to curse. So, be careful.

As we transition from the **Why** to the **What** of soul health, I'm sure you're wondering why I didn't recognize this or that uniqueness or danger of ministry. Believe me, what I've covered here in this chapter is the tip of the iceberg. I know there was much left unsaid or emphasized. But I just couldn't take it anymore. As the author, I've triggered my own PTSP; and, as the reader, I suspect you have, too. We both need to move on. Let's rise from the ash heap where we've been scratching our Jobian wounds and turn our eyes heavenward to where our help comes from.

So, where do we go from here? The rest of this book is dedicated to robust principles, dispositions, and interventions for ministers engaged in a unique and dangerous professional calling; however, before we get to the **What** of ministerial soul health, a foundation of nobility is called for.

25. Portal, *How to be (Un)Successful*, 27.

The Uniqueness and Danger of Ministry

While ministry is unique and dangerous, it is simultaneously the noblest and most important work on earth. The nobility of professional ministry lays the foundation for the ministerial soul health **Why**.

The Nobility of Ministry

If a commission by an earthly king is considered an honor, how can a commission by a Heavenly King be considered a sacrifice?[26]

—David Livingstone, Scottish Physician and Missionary

What an honor we feel when someone of significance and perhaps authority selects us to join them in a task. Starting small, have you ever been picked for a team on the recess ground? It feels good to be picked, that is, if you're not last, of course. Imagine the leader of your denomination picking you out among many to be a part of the few given a unique and most important task for your tribe. Imagine a senator, governor, president, or king anointing you for the most crucial task. Indeed, you can sense the noble feeling accompanying such an appointment.

Now, permit yourself to imagine this appointment or anointing coming from the King of kings and Lord of lords. The God of the universe has selected you from his many to be a part of his few, and you are given by God the task of directly influencing human souls for all of eternity. Again, as I said before, all work is sacred when offered to God. However, not all work directly addresses the eternal disposition of human souls. I would argue that only the divinely called, professional, anointed minister in ministry is the singular most important vocation on the face of the earth.

Consider how Charles Spurgeon, a great preacher, put it:

> He that can toy with his ministry and count it to be like a trade, or like any other profession, was never called of God. But he that has a charge pressing on his heart, and a woe ringing in his ear, and preaches as though he heard the cries of hell behind him, and saw his God looking down on him, oh, how that man begs the Lord that his hearers may not hear in vain![27]

---

26. Piper, "I Never Made a Sacrifice."
27. Spurgeon, "He That Can Toy."

The Why of Ministerial Soul Health

Goodness, fellow ministers. I'm sure you, like me, have strained and wept over many sermons, delivering each like a mother in labor, begging God to deliver those from the darkness of hell's womb to the marvelous light of God's family, affecting the eternal trajectory of human souls hearing your voice.

Wow! What a unique vocational work of the divinely called minister. Take a moment and permit yourself to bask in that nobility.

Back to the weighty work of ministry. Perhaps this weight is why Paul identified the preaching ministry of word and doctrine to Timothy as "labor" (1 Tim 5:17). I'm sure, much like you, we have strained in preaching to see many delivered from eternal darkness to eternal light as some kind of soul birthing labor. What other professional vocation bears this eternal weight? A cardiologist I know told me that they often have temporal life and death literally in their hands, but he never sensed that he had eternal life and death in his hands, as a preacher must feel. Does an accountant weep over the eternal nature of their spreadsheet? Does an engineer feel the eternal weight of their building design? Does a truck driver believe that the product he's delivering will save someone from eternal torment? Perhaps, if they're hauling Bibles, I suppose, as unlikely as that is. But I digress.

Consider this passage from Acts 20:28: "Therefore take heed to yourselves and to all the flock, among which the Holy Spirit has made you overseers, to shepherd the church of God which He purchased with His own blood." Apparently, to God, the most valuable currency in the universe, His Son's blood, was spent to purchase the church. Therefore, the universal Christian church (those who consider Christ their King) is the most important organization on earth, the supreme nation, if you will. And you ministers have been commissioned and anointed by the heavenly King as professional ordained leaders of that nation. Please take a moment to pause and permit yourself to feel the nobility of such a mantle.

Can you find that sense of nobility in you? Perhaps it's been buried in the context of this twenty-first century cultural moment of flagging trust and appreciation of the local pastor. Andrew Root states, "We live in a time—call it a secular age—when society has devalued the pastor, yet we nevertheless yearn for ministry." He further recognizes the recent research confirming our postmodern context:

> For sixteen straight years, nurses, and not clergy, have topped the Gallup poll of the most trusted professions in America. Eighty-two percent of people said that nurses were trustworthy. Only

The Uniqueness and Danger of Ministry

42 percent trusted clergy or pastors. Police officers, grade school teachers, and pharmacists ranked higher in trust, honesty, and ethics than pastors.[28]

Dr. Fred Garmon of LeaderLabs, which targets leadership formation in professional ministers, reports that after surveying six thousand graduates from LeaderLabs, over 80 percent state that if they could easily and seamlessly transition to another vocation, they would. Dr. Garmon also declares that ministry burnout is at epidemic levels.[29]

Can you access the seminal nobility of your calling to ministry amidst this postmodern ministry malaise? You must if you want to carry on the blessing and burden inherent to professional ministry. Once again, I'm begging you to take a moment right now to pause and permit yourself to feel the nobility of such a mantle. Ask the Holy Spirit to recover in you the joy from the moment you knew it pleased God to anoint you as a watchman on the wall and shepherd of his people.

The eternal destiny and quality of souls is the work of professional ministry. No other temporal professional vocation bears this kind of weight. Therefore, make it your pastoral passion to be the healthiest minister you can be, for the **Why** of ministry is simultaneously founded on its nobility, yet acutely aware and vigilant regarding its uniqueness and danger. Let's turn our attention from the **Why** of ministerial soul health to the **What** of ministerial soul health.

Achtung! Before we move on, stop guessing and start assessing!

I don't know who said "Stop guessing and start assessing" originally, but I like it. As a minister, I am intrinsically tempted to guess at my church discipleship competence, assimilation success, the current state of congregational health, my soul health, and so on. As my old friend Richard used to say, "Human beings have an unlimited capacity for self-delusion."[30] From one self-deluded minister to another, don't guess about your or your church's soul health; assess it.

When you visit your physician, they typically take your vitals and other health metrics. This holistic exam normally includes nine items:

---

28. Root, *Pastor in a Secular Age*, xix.

29. Fred Garmon, stated during a primer speech at the seminal committee meeting for The Institute of Leadership Formation, January 3, 2024.

30. Richard P. Mied, PhD, stated many times during our long friendship and self-published posthumously by his family in *Mied's Laws*. I miss that dude.

temperature, weight, blood pressure, pulse, gland status, gut organ rigidity, reflexes, breathing, and oxygenation. Exams such as these use these nine items to determine the current state of physical health and assess health trends. That makes sense, right? Well, why don't we do something similar with our soul and the soul of our church, life group, marriage, etc.?

Below are the nine vital signs of soul health provided by the apostle Paul in Gal 5:22. Following this list will be a short soul exam. Now, you wouldn't visit your physician and tell them that you have already assessed your vital signs and, by self-assessment, announce that you are as physically fit as a fiddle. Does anyone know why a fiddle is the benchmark for being fit physically? Anyway, you wouldn't do that with your doctor, so why do it with yourself and your church?

For integrity's sake, don't take this exam yourself. Give this exam to your spouse or a trusted friend who will be honest. I'm taking my cue from Prov 27:6, espousing that the wounds of a friend are faithful and far more valuable than false flattery from an enemy. If it's a friend, make sure they know you and know that honesty is the only way this kind of exam could be helpful. Tell them you are counting on them to be clinically honest. My hunch is that you've got a better chance of getting unvarnished honesty from a friend than a spouse. I mean, you have to live with your spouse. So, use wisdom here. After the spouse or friend has assessed you on the nine soul-health vital signs, plan to meet and discuss the results openly.

The exam metrics are the nine soul health vital signs (Gal 5:22): love, joy, peace, patience, kindness, goodness, faithfulness, gentleness, and self-control. Here are the holistic soul exam questions as if the one being examined is asking their examiner:

- Would loving be in the top one or two ways you would describe me to others who don't know me?

    Not at all 1......3......5......7......10 Absolutely

- Am I clearly a joyful person?

    Not at all 1......3......5......7......10 Absolutely

- Does the word peaceful come to mind as a top descriptor when you think of me?

    Not at all 1......3......5......7......10 Absolutely

The Uniqueness and Danger of Ministry

- Do you find me to be a patient person?

    Not at all 1......3......5......7......10 Absolutely

- Are you confident that the trait of kindness would be a top characteristic most people think of when they think of me?

    Not at all 1......3......5......7......10 Absolutely

- When you think of me, does goodness rise to the top of the ways you would describe me?

    Not at all 1......3......5......7......10 Absolutely

- Do you consider me a faithful person?

    Not at all 1......3......5......7......10 Absolutely

- Do you think of gentleness when you think of me?

    Not at all 1......3......5......7......10 Absolutely

- Am I a self-controlled person?

    Not at all 1......3......5......7......10 Absolutely

    Don't move on until you do this exam and process the results!

2

The *What* of Ministerial Soul Health

The exclusive work of the professional minister is to shepherd the eternal souls of human beings toward the fullness of their original humanness in the image of God.

But what is the anatomy of an original, eternal soul?

IN THIS CHAPTER, I'M not interested in surveying historical theories regarding the nature of a soul. I'm also not competing against any other historical or contemporary sense of what a soul is. In this chapter, I aim to offer a holistic vision of the soul, one that is both relevant and practical for both ministers and members, which most readers will intuitively find appealing in their everyday lives. Mind you, the word "holistic" is the keyword for soul health in this chapter.

First, let's consider Matt 16:24–26. Contextually, Jesus is characterizing his final days as a required all-in commitment for him. He extends an invitation to his disciples of this all-in commitment, which will soon require an all-in cost, so to speak, if they continue to follow him during and after his sacrifice.

Then Jesus said to his disciples, "If any of you wants to be my follower, you must give up your own way, take up your cross, and follow me. If you try to hold onto your *life* [*psuche*], you will lose it. But if you give up your *life* [*psuche*] for my sake, you will save it. And what do you benefit if you gain the whole world but lose your own *soul* [*psuche*]? Is anything worth more than your *soul* [*psuche*]?"[1]

I'm in no way minimizing the all-in sacrifice that following Jesus demands. We indeed lay down our whole life to follow Jesus, or we don't follow him at all. There is no minimizing the all-in life sacrifice following Jesus requires. However, note in the passage the two different English words, "life" and "soul," and the single Greek word, *psuche*, which is used for both "life" and "soul." Jesus here talks about life and soul as if they are the same. Life is soul, and soul is life. The ultimate exemplar of humanness, Jesus, toggles life and soul as the same. Our whole soul is our whole life.

The principle I overlooked for many years as a young Christian was this concept of soul and life integration. For instance, I lived as if my thought life was segregated into the sacred and secular realms. If I were contemplating spiritual matters, such as prayer or a theological principle, that would be a sacred thought. However, if I were thinking about changing the alternator in my car, that would be a secular thought. Put another way, my feelings at church were sacred, and my feelings while playing or watching sports were secular feelings. Although I believe thoughts and feelings concerning sports can be sanctified, I simply didn't regard my feelings while watching or playing sports as something that required the attentiveness of my soul. Those thoughts and feelings had nothing to do with my soul.

Furthermore, my body was also disintegrated. I didn't recognize my body as part of my soul. Now, of course, I did recognize my body as part of my soul if I was sinning with my body, such as sexually, but strangely not if I was making a sandwich or driving my car. I passively accepted without question the Greco-Roman anthropological ethos in which I was born, which stated that my earthly life and my heavenly life had little to do with each other, except for worship attendance and sinful behavior modification. The soul was something to be saved and, by and large, set on a shelf to await that great day when I take it down and have St. Peter at the pearly gates scan its barcode, hoping it registers as saved. My soul had little to do with my everyday walking-around life, and my physical life had little overlap with my spiritual soul. Therefore, even though I knew Paul admonished every Christ follower to glorify God in the basics of sustaining human life, eating and drinking (1 Cor 10:31), I didn't consider eating Doritos or a doughnut

---

1. Matt 16:24–26, emphasis and Greek added.

a soul event. Consequently, I missed Jesus' point in the Gospel, which is the danger of living a disintegrated life.

Richard Foster's brief article on "Salvation as a Life" effectively summarizes the notion that I think Jesus is conveying in the passage above from Matt 16.[2] Foster advocates for proclaiming a gospel salvation that is for all of life, or *zoë*. This vision of life (*zoë*) encompasses everything related to creation, including prayer, household chores, worship, sex, work, Bible reading, meal preparation, serving, driving, and other daily activities. Therefore, when John declares that God so loved the world (cosmos), he sent his only Son to save it, he meant precisely that, everything. Jesus came to save everything. Salvation is not for a soul as something that sits on a shelf waiting to have its barcode scanned by St. Peter at the pearly gates. No, salvation is for a soul, a life, *psuche*, *zoë*, everything. Foster harkens to the wisdom of Willard in that God is not interested in your spiritual life. God is interested in your life.

In Matt 16, Jesus offers us a holistic view of the soul, which I intend to describe textually and visually in the balance of this chapter. In addition to holistic soul integration, I will address the ancient sacred/secular or spiritual/physical disintegration in more detail. Finally, I will address a few critical impediments to integrating soul health. Much of the following draws from Dallas Willard's concept of a holistic soul, as presented in his book *Renovation of the Heart*.[3] For a more in-depth exploration of the soul, I highly recommend you engage Willard on this matter.

Anatomy of the Soul

The **What** of soul health is predicated on a solid understanding of what a soul is. John Ortberg offers the following vision of what a soul is in its essential function: "The soul is that aspect of your whole being that correlates, integrates, and enlivens everything going on in the various dimensions of the self. The soul is the life center of human beings."[4]

For ministers, the what of soul health, the anatomy of the soul, is a foundational concept and lived reality; it must be. Ministers are soul shepherds. How can a soul shepherd effectively shepherd if they don't know what a soul is and how it was designed to function? I operated for decades

---

2. Foster, "Salvation as a Life."
3. Willard, *Renovation of the Heart*, 31.
4. Ortberg, *Soul Keeping*, 35.

as a minister assuming but not knowing what a soul was and how it was intended to function. I was an ignorant soul shepherd.

The people whom God draws to us for soul shepherding expect that we know what we're doing. The problem is that the minister is a soul, too, in need of shepherding. We are shepherding souls while at the same time being shepherded by the Good Shepherd. Consequently, ministers must be solidly in command of three things: one, what a soul is; two, how it is designed by God to function; and three, a lived expertise in soul-centered living.

I'm a surfer. When I go to surf a new spot, I want local knowledge. I want to know that I'm being guided by someone who lives near and surfs the place often. I want a surf shepherd. Once this surf shepherd trains me in surfing the spot, I can then become a surf shepherd for someone else. In other words, I don't want a tourist as a tour guide.

When ministers attempt to lead souls somewhere they don't live, it is the lost leading the lost. Or, as Jesus put it in Matt 15:14 and Luke 6:39, the blind leading the blind. As a soul shepherd, you can't lead someone somewhere you don't live. Soul shepherding is qualified by the successfully lived soul experience of the shepherd, to greater or lesser degrees. What I mean by that is Jesus never expected soul-shepherding ministers to be perfect souls, but he certainly meant that you're not posing as a soul-shepherd.

Before a soul shepherd can lead souls to the kingdom of God and teach them how to live there, they must first live there and understand how to live there. This lived experience begins with those who are called to soul shepherding knowing their soul and how it was designed to operate. So, let's start the **What** of soul health with, well, what a soul is and how it works.

Going forward, I will develop the anatomy of the soul using concentric circles to convey the idea that the soul has an epicenter that emanates influence outward and receives influence inward, thereby moving through all other dimensions of the soul. The soul's will is at the center of the soul and the chief determinant of soul health.

My primary presupposition is that original human creation came with the capacity to choose. The fact that God has a will and the original human, created in God's image, also has a will is a given here. Therefore, before Gen 3, original humans surrendered their will to God's will, reaping the benefits of fully living in the fullness of their original identity as beings who love God, themselves, and others. Thereby, God's will be done on earth as in heaven. A world of perfection and integration, where humans defer to God's will rather than their own, yields perfect harmony among humans, between humans and God, and between humans and nature. This pervasive harmony is what Jesus prayed in the high priestly prayer of John 17. Romans 8 says the world is groaning to return to this perfect integration of all created things and the Creator.

Groaning for a return because, of course, in Gen 3, humanity chose to surrender to its own will rather than God's. This choice disintegrated the world. This disintegration results from original sin, namely, surrendering to an inappropriate authority. Another presupposition about the will here is that it is not designed to rule but to surrender to be ruled. The human will was not created to muster power but to surrender to power. Ideally, surrender to the proper control of the Creator, but surrender to power just the same. Therefore, humans don't need will-power to live as they were originally designed to live; they need will-surrender. What we humans surrender to is what we empower to rule us. We were originally designed to be ruled by the Spirit, counterintuitively empowering our surrender to be fruitful and multiply perfectly. In other words, surrendering to the proper power of the Holy Spirit is empowering to live the abundant life we were originally created to live.

Jesus is, of course, our model. I often need to be reminded of his words in John 8:29, "I only do those things that please the Father." How about Luke 22:42, "I want your will to be done, not mine"? Or, consider the forerunner of Jesus, John the Baptist in John 3:30, "He must increase and I must decrease." Then, on into the Epistles, with Paul declaring a model of being to the Galatians: "It is no longer I who live, but Christ who lives in me" (Gal 2:20). This exhortation is possessive language. Paul encourages being possessed by Christ's Spirit in such a way that we become obedient, like a shadow. This invitation to oneness with Jesus and the Father, as he prays in John 17, is an invitation to the radical, transformative gospel call to become a new species, from sinner to saint. Furthermore, according to the model of Jesus and the admonitions of John and Paul, this holistic sanctification is not attained by will-power but by will-surrender. But be mindful, pastor, we cannot lead here if we do not live here.

By the way, I did mean to use the word "species" above. I am convinced that the comprehensive, holistic, immersive Christian conversion experience is, in fact, a transformation from one species, a sinner, to another, a saint. In other places, I've written academically about Hebraic anthropology, which stands in stark contrast to Greek anthropology, a perspective deeply ingrained in Western culture. In short, the Hebraic anthropological exegesis of Gen 2:7 leads to the conclusion that the human species is only human when animated by the Spirit's breath of God. In Gen 3, we got the breath knocked out of us by sin, and at that cataclysmic moment, we humans were transformed into something other than human. Originally, human meant being animated by and living in the power of the Spirit's breath. Being born again, as Jesus characterizes in John 3, is being positionally transformed back into our original human essence. Sanctification is the practical work of learning how to live as we were originally intended to live. But I digress.

Surrender to the will of the Spirit results in soul health, yet surrender to any other power than the Spirit leads to soul disease or sinfulness. The great challenge to every minister as a soul shepherd is leading souls out of the bondage of humanism, where the self-will is the supreme authority, into the freedom of surrender to the Spirit in the kingdom of God where all things increasingly fall into place (Matt 6:33). However, if a minister isn't increasingly living in the freedom of surrender to the Spirit's authority as in the areas of money, humor, entertainment, eating, sex inside and outside of marriage, fantasy, internet browsing, attitude, emotional regulation, humility, and so on, that soul shepherd is a blind guide. We can only lead people to where we live. So, consider the slides that follow as your soul's description and prescription, not as fodder for preaching and teaching for other souls. Start and restart with your soul. This process of starting and restarting (the cycle of repentance) is the essence of Spirit-empowered sanctification, extending to all of life, the sacred and the secular. Onward!

In this concentric anatomy of the soul, the will is synonymous with the human spirit, lowercase "s." Therefore, the center of the human soul is where a person's spirit interacts, integrates, and becomes one with the Holy Spirit. Ecclesiastes 3:11 offers a profound insight when the author informs us that our Creator has planted eternity in the human heart from the beginning. Therefore, human life as originally intended by the Creator emanates from this center of the soul, surrendering to the Spirit. Jesus put it this way in Matt 6:33, "Seek first the kingdom of God and all these things will be added to you." When we get the first thing right, the rest falls into place.

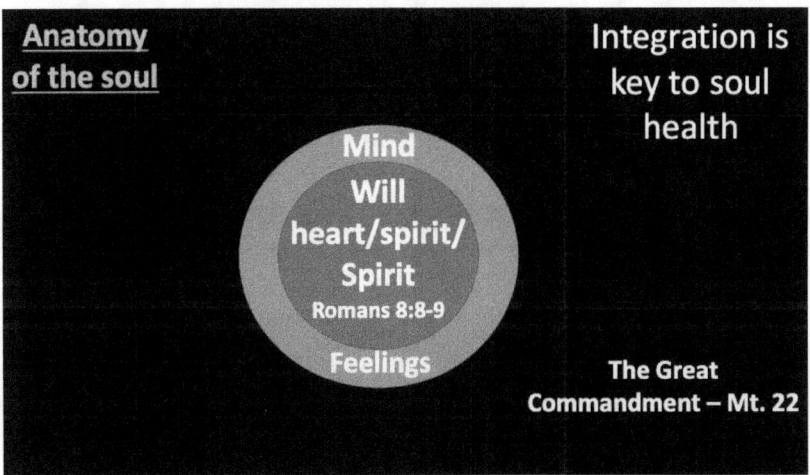

Keeping our focus on the pre-fall person's soul, the next circle of influence emanating outward from the center includes the mind, thoughts, and emotions. Once again, it is a post-fall tendency in Western culture to disintegrate the mind and feelings from the soul, except in selectively sinful areas. You likely have admonished yourself or others to be wary of following our heart and not our head, or vice versa. Imagining, thinking, and feeling as two different dimensions of humanness is disintegrating.

Considering pre-fall integration, imagine the human will wholly surrender to the proper authority of God as Creator, emanating outward to a mind taking captive every thought to the obedience of Christ and the feelings of peace that pass all understanding, even in a post-fall world. When we do this, we can begin to imagine the original integration and perhaps even live it. This imagination provides our vision of original human flourishing. Living this integration makes Christ's incarnation real in this cultural moment.

Rather than focusing on mustering the willpower to strong-arm our thoughts and feelings into submission, original creation invites surrender instead of power. Of course, the key to this integration resulting in increasing holistic peace is surrender to the proper authority rather than surrender to the improper authority. Improper authority is anything other than the Spirit. Said differently, identifying the competing authorities, typically the Spirit and the self, in everything from eating and drinking, staying up later than usual, buying or not buying anything, running for political office, or getting married, is a nurtured skill of the soul. Training in the soul skill of surrender to the proper authority will be the difference between soul health and soul disease.

Try this right now. Beyond fight or flight due to being chased by a bear or burglar, bring to mind something non-fight or flight that is stealing peace from your soul. Track the feeling to a thought that surrenders to an improper authority, such as fear of something outside you. For example, not succeeding at work, an offense you've internalized by someone you thought was your friend, declining attendance at church, or a child getting on your last nerve. Yes, these are all examples of improper external authorities we consistently surrender to, resulting in all manner of anxiety, depression, anger, and other peace-stealing slavery.

Consider the truth: beyond flight or fight events, neither anyone nor anything can force you to think or feel something mentally or emotionally. Let that sink in. No one is to blame for your thoughts or feelings other than you. You own you! It's all in the surrender.

How often have you said, "I can't believe they said that to me. That makes me so mad." Or, "She really hurt me when she said . . ." Or, "The war in Ukraine makes me so nervous." Or, "This election has me so upset, what if _____ gets in office? Oh, my goodness, I just couldn't handle it."

Yeah, me too. I've spent much of my life believing that everyone and everything except me was responsible for my thoughts and emotions. This psychosis is a surrender to an improper authority. Viktor Frankl makes this plain in his book *Man's Search for Meaning*, where he recounts his experience in a German concentration camp. I mean, seriously, who can trump the card of a concentration camp survivor? Over time, Frankl recognizes that the resilience of prisoners is directly correlated with their surrender. Those who surrendered mentally and emotionally to the authority of German soldiers and the camp conditions unraveled in resilience, dying quickly. However, those who did not surrender mentally or emotionally to the authority of German soldiers or camp conditions strengthened in resilience, seeming to thrive. No doubt that German soldiers could cause physical pain, and camp conditions were often deadly; however, prisoners who did not surrender to the mental and emotional pressure of the German soldiers or camp conditions increased in resilience. Frankl posited that a human being can endure any what or how as long as they have a robust why.[5] The human will was created to surrender to the proper authority of the Holy Spirit, not the human spirit.

One other poignant story on the principle of surrender comes from the life of musician Bob Dylan. When Dylan transitioned from folk to rock music in the late 1960s, his purist folk music fans expressed betrayal. These folk fans grew increasingly antagonistic at concerts where Dylan was performing. Fans were quite happy during the first acoustic folk set, but when Dylan transitioned to the rock and roll of the second set, the fans expressed their discontent by yelling condemnation toward him on stage. In one instance, an audience member screamed "Judas," associating Dylan with the quintessential biblical example of betrayal. Dylan approached the mic and emphatically declared, "I don't believe you."[6] With this simple retort, Dylan rebuked the detractor; instead of surrendering to the irate audience member's belief, he surrendered to his conviction about himself. This response was a matter of the will, empowering the mind and setting at peace the emotions.

Imagine how you would posture yourself toward your detractors. Imagine someone declares a negative opinion about you in a leadership/staff meeting, on the highway, in your kitchen, to a church member, or more likely on social media, and you surrender to God's positive opinion about you rather than their negative one. This choice is the power of surrendering to the Spirit rather than the spirit. Neither anyone nor anything can force you to think or feel something.

5. Frankl, *Man's Search for Meaning*, 137–66.
6. Gleadow, "Perfect Four-Word Response," 9.

Of course, in contrast to my history of empowering others to make me think and feel negatively, I curiously owned all my good thoughts and feelings. For instance, have you ever heard someone declare, "That makes me so compassionate." Or, "Oh, I really don't want to be kind, but they make me so kind." Right, you and I have never heard such a thing. I love taking credit for my positive thoughts and feelings, but sadly, blaming others and circumstances for my negative thoughts and feelings has been the history of my soul. The reality is that our thoughts and feelings reference the center of our soul, where our will either surrenders to the Spirit of God or the spirit of the world. We become slaves to that which we surrender to.

Back to Frankl's wisdom, he is often quoted as saying, "Between stimulus and response lies a space. In that space lie both our freedom and power to choose a response. In our response lies our growth and happiness, or our atrophy and disturbance."[7] Perhaps this is best seen in Jesus on the cross when, against all odds and in the face of quintessential injustice, he forgives those crucifying him because he chose to. No one made him feel compassion, forgiveness, hatred, love, or bitterness; he decided to be who he was created to be and live as he was created to live, doing the will of his Father on earth as it is in heaven. Repossessing power by surrendering to God's will is also how Paul can say in Rom 12:18, "As much as it depends on you, live at peace with all people." You own you. Modeling this before your spouse, children, and congregation is how you lead people to the repossession of their soul's power. The epicenter of the soul's power is the will, which flows out into the mind, influencing our feelings.

One more time, before we move outward to the next circle of the soul, imagine a will wholly surrendered to the Spirit. Surrendering to the Spirit begets a mind captivated by Christ, and the peace that passes all understanding will naturally follow from following the Prince of Peace. This ripple effect then flows into the body.

---

7. Vesley, "Alleged Quote."

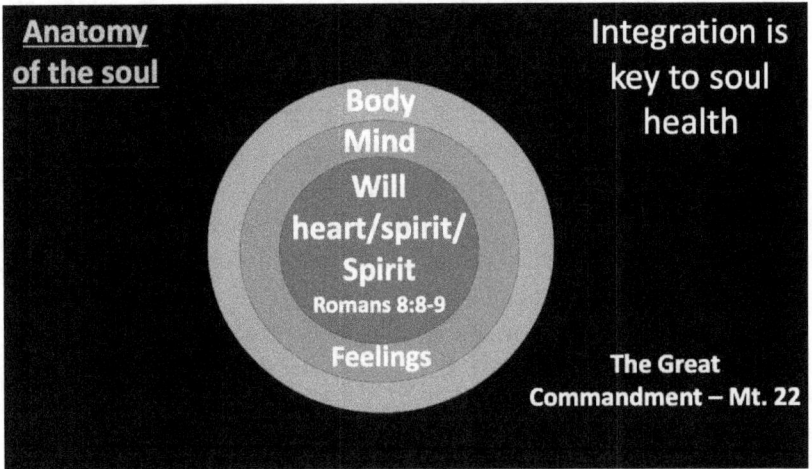

In the body, integration or disintegration of the will, mind, and feelings is viscerally felt and expressed. When we surrender to the proper authority (our Creator, who loves us) and begin thinking as that authority wills, we feel confident and at peace, which translates to a relaxed body that is physiologically at peace. When we surrender to an improper authority (a created entity that does not love us) and begin thinking like that nefarious entity wills, we feel anxious and fearful, which translates to a tense body that is dis-eased physiologically.

You know the sensation of integration, or the lack thereof, intuitively. When your will or spirit is surrendered to the Spirit, your mind is more apt to take captive every thought to the obedience of Christ, resulting in feelings of peace that are physiologically experienced in your body. The negative inverse of integration is disintegration, resulting in anxiety and depression, resulting in the exact opposite of integration's result. Contemporary science marks the harmful effects of a disintegrated, anxious, and depressed life orientation.[8]

The temptation here is to imagine that a genuinely relaxed, non-anxious person has a set of external circumstances that allow them to relax, such as having plenty of money, power, approval from the right people, security in their work, and appreciation from those closest and most influential in their life. This external orientation is not the orientation of the holistically integrated soul I'm advocating here. The biblical Christo-formed soul does not experience soul peace from the outside but from the inside.

8. Bryan, "God, Can I Tell You Something?"

In other words, the Christo-formed integrated soul is at peace, independent of external circumstances.

While on a mission trip with my church in Haiti, we needed water to mix concrete, and the only source was a stream located up a steep path on the dry, desert-like mountainside. Carrying our buckets up the narrow path, I was startled to see a man lying near a very green garden, four feet by eight feet in size, full of what looked like thriving plants. I recognized the man from the desperately poor village in the riverbed below, whom I'd seen often walking near our project, always singing and smiling. When we passed him, he shouted, "Greetings, my friends. May the Lord bless you in life as He's blessed me."

In my Western, first-world estimation, nothing external in the man's life could produce the peace and joy ostensibly present inside him. In this pitiful place of external human suffering, an internal, pervasive sense of peace and joy was present, emanating outward from a will surrendered to the kingdom of God and the Prince of Peace. Yet, in my prosperous place of external human flourishing (America), an internal pervasive sense of anxiety and depression was present, emanating outward from a will surrendered to the kingdom of the world and the prince of darkness.

A non-anxious presence does not come from the outside but from the inside. Nothing outside of us can produce peace that God originally created inside of us. It starts with our will surrendering to the Spirit. It continues with our minds being renewed by the mind of Christ, as our feelings follow in the current of peace beyond all understanding, resulting in a body that is relaxed and peaceful, regardless of external circumstances. This witness of the original, holistically integrated pre-Gen 3 human life has the most robust potential to positively influence our social relationships.

The What of Ministerial Soul Health

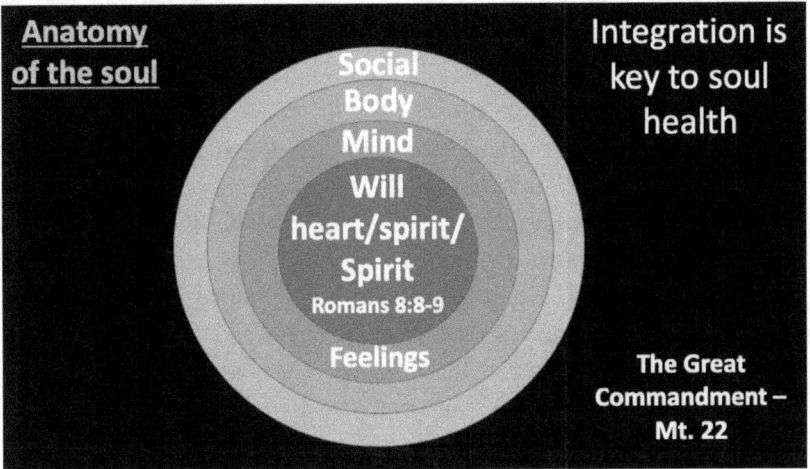

In both original and redeemed creation, the social realm of the soul serves as the outlet for the power of positive influence emanating from the integrated epicenter of the soul. Here is the great power of professional ministers to have either a positive or negative impact on the people of God. From the wellspring of a minister's soul surrendered to the will of the Spirit, through a mind captive to Christ and emotions anchored in a peace that transcends understanding, flows joy and peace into their social relationships. Conversely, from the wellspring of a minister's soul surrendered to the will of the self, through a mind captive to the carnal and emotions anchored in anxiety, flows defensiveness and discontentment into their social relationships. The greatest gift a minister can give their congregation is a secure, non-anxious presence.

Hold on here. I've gotten ahead of myself. The most crucial place of influence for the professional minister is not the people of God in their church but the people of God in their family. Imagine living a life free from anxiety in the presence of your spouse and children. This circle of social influence is at the internal edge of the social ring of the soul in our diagram. Only from the social influence of the minister's family can the minister extend influence to the church they lead. Therefore, the foundational influence of an integrated or disintegrated soul will be the minister's family. Consequently, the greatest gift a minister can give their family is a secure, non-anxious presence. I will address the subject of ministerial family health in more detail later; however, consider the minister's social influence within

The Uniqueness and Danger of Ministry

the community they serve, starting with their family, extending to their church family, and beyond.

There is no vocational leadership position more recognized as holistically influential than the minister. Consider the military general. Who would imagine this leader as the quintessential model for sexual purity or familial fidelity, but a pastor is? Consider the CEO of any company. Who would consider this leader the quintessential model for marital health, yet the pastor is regarded as the marriage standard simply by the title? Consider the airplane pilot. Who would look to this leader as the quintessential model for parenting advice, yet the pastor is? Consider a politician. Who would consider this leader the quintessential model for honesty, yet the pastor is?

In a 360-degree expectation reality, the minister is the quintessential model for a holistically healthy life in any community. The minister's social influence is comprehensive. Of course, it's irrational for anyone to expect comprehensive ministerial influence completely. However, it is the reality that every minister lives with: a 360-degree scrutiny regarding every area of life, from their speech to their attitude on the sports pitch, to how much they eat or drink, what entertainment they take in, how fast or slow they drive, the clothes they wear in the park or pulpit, how their kids behave, to the way they vote. This comprehensive influence is a crushing burden in a broken world where the minister is likely chief among all the sinners in their charge. In addition to this, the pressure of pastoral performance is assessed every Sunday, presenting a daunting challenge. Again, as I stated in the first chapter, this vocational crucible is a reality, not because the minister is doing anything wrong. Wraparound ministerial influence and expectation are inherent to professional ministry.

The only "soul-u-tion" is to embrace an inside-out vision of holistic soul health. A solution that starts with the epicenter of a will surrendered to the Spirit, resulting in a mind captivated by the mind of Christ, leading to feelings of peace that pass all understanding, experienced in a relaxed body living from rest, not restlessness, thereby flowing into all social relationships where the contagious soul health of the integrated minister infects all under their influence as the quintessential model of a fully redeemed non-anxious human soul. Now, that's a good run-on sentence right there!

Consider the wisdom of esteemed psychological and leadership guru Edwin Freeman, as presented in his classic book *A Failure of Nerve*. He emphasizes the power of a non-anxious presence in any system, from a family, to a church, to a nation. "Clearly defined, non-anxious leadership promotes healthy differentiation throughout a system, while reactive, peace-at-all-costs, anxious leadership does the opposite."[9]

Being that Friedman is Jewish, it's hard to read his book without imagining that, underlying the supreme principle he espouses—a non-anxious presence—as the ultimate leadership quality, is drawn from his vision of Jehovah, the God of the Bible. Representing a non-anxious God to God's people is the minister's privilege and problem. The minister's soul is a model of the soul of God, represented visually to humanity in the form of his son Jesus Christ, the visible image of the invisible God. The minister is the visible image of the invisible Christ.

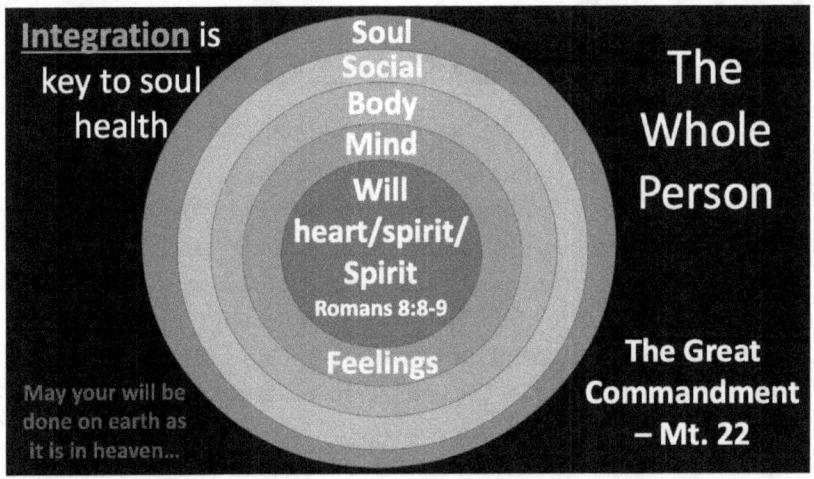

This slide gives us a visual **What** of soul health: the integrated soul. As stated at the beginning of this chapter, I'm not interested in debating theological constructs of a human soul. I am, however, interested in offering a vision of the human soul that may intuitively make sense as an integrated whole. I'm sure more components could be factored into the concentric circles. The symmetry and synergy of the integrated original human soul, in contrast to the disintegrated soul of original sin, is what I'm trying to convey here. The following disintegrated image is intended to be juxtaposed with the previous integrated image.

9. Friedman, *Failure of Nerve*, 273.

The Uniqueness and Danger of Ministry

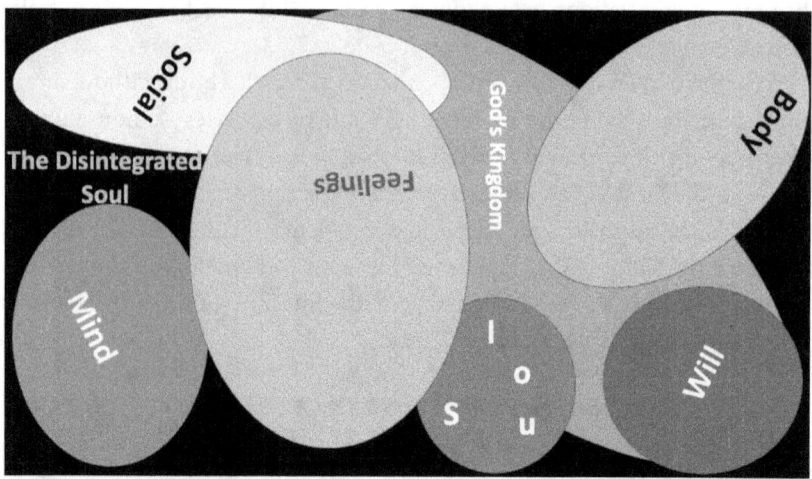

The slide above provides a visual of a soul disintegrated, disoriented, and therefore disordered due to sinfulness. If Gen 3's sinfulness is the opposite of Gen 1 and 2's wholeness, our only hope is for the Creator to intervene. Thankfully, he did this with a vision and provision. The holistically healthy vision of a human soul in a holistically broken world is the image of Jesus Christ (John 1, Phil 2). The provision is that, by the power of death and resurrection, this same Jesus Christ can live in us, raising us from the death of disintegration to the life of integration (Rom 8:11).

Sadly, many Christian ministers and, consequently, Christians live with saved but disintegrated, disheveled souls. A disheveled or disordered soul is a soul tormented by all that is outside. Rather than projecting peace and joy from inside out to the world (Rom 14:17), the disintegrated soul receives anxiety and discontent from the outside world and internalizes it. Jesus provided for the reintegration of the soul. Being born again means being restored to our original state of integration. This soul-disordered condition does not need to be; a new vision of the human soul is necessary. One that reorients us to the need for integration from the inside out. Let's look at the formational direction in the following few slides.

The What of Ministerial Soul Health

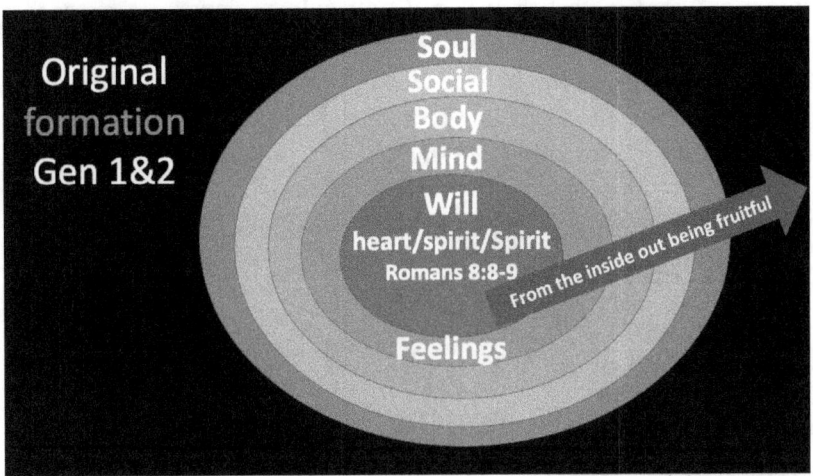

Jesus, in Matt 6, stated that the epicenter of human flourishing is the person seeking the kingdom of God first. After this surrender, all the other things we get so wrapped around the axle about will fall into place. Sequencing our soul is critical, yet not complicated. It all begins with the soul's center, the will. From here, holistic health naturally ripples out as originally intended from the soul's center. Soul health flows sequentially out from the center into and through the expanding realms of the soul. This flow is the direction of the original formation. This flow is being fruitful and multiplying now as intended in Eden.

A will/spirit surrender to the Spirit's will naturally results in a mind captivated by the mind of Christ, which leads naturally to a peaceful disposition beyond any broken human understanding, resulting in a physical body relaxed and at ease rather than dis-eased. Ultimately, this inside-out flow naturally extends to all social relationships, allowing for the experience and expression of a holistically healthy soul. Another way to envision this is the familiar adage of getting the horse in front of the cart. The horse is our will, and the cart is everything else. When we expect peace to come from the cart (external circumstances) to the horse (internal center), we have it all backwards.

A natural, externally generalized result of this inside-out directional flow is the health and well-being of all creation. In partnership with the Creator, humans were intended to be co-caretakers of creation (Gen 1:28). Therefore, from the original human will into the world flowed the will of God done on earth as it is in heaven. This flow is original to the directional vision of Gen 1–2, that the will of God would be done on earth as it is in heaven through human beings. Anything less than this original, inside-out flow of God's will through the human will into the world is unnatural. Genesis 3 marks the beginning of a misdirected flow of will, leading to disintegration, disorder, and deformation.

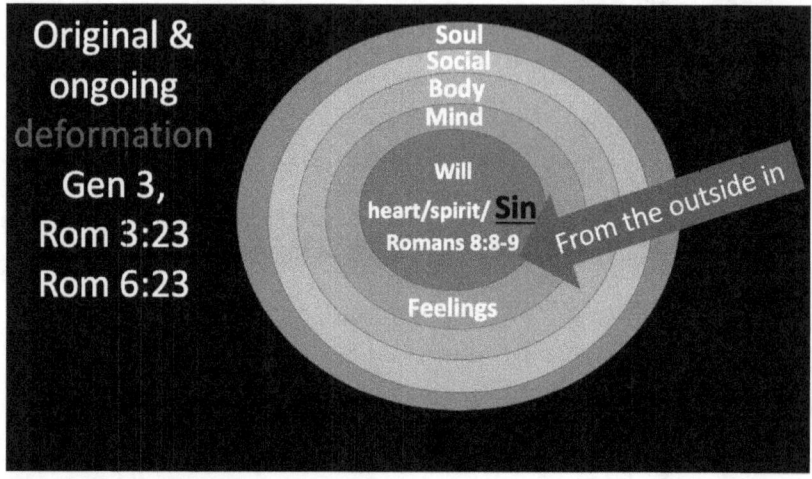

In Rom 3–8, we have a vision of how, since Gen 3, that which is outside of us, beginning with the external influence of the snake, has deformed us from the outside in. Consequently, our will is preoccupied with external entities, circumstances, and concerns. This external circumstantial flow enters our soul generally through social relationships, stressing our bodies, poisoning our minds and feelings as our will surrenders to the nefarious pseudo-authority of what is outside of us—this capitulation to external authorities dis-eases our soul. We need an intervention. We need to be born again.

The What of Ministerial Soul Health

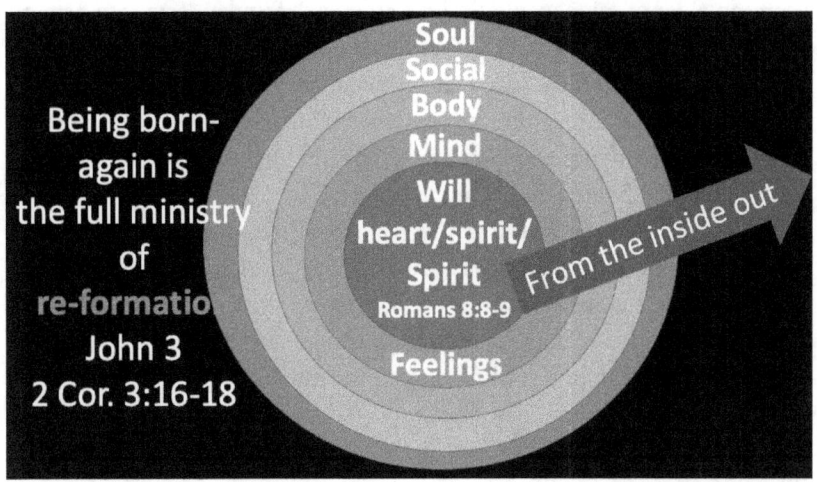

From an evangelical perspective, it is understood that the salvation experience begins with the Spirit's draw (planted there in the human heart according to Eccl 3:11), human surrender as repentance to this drawing (Rom 10:10), the Spirit redeeming and converting the sinner's soul to a saint's soul (2 Cor 3:16–18), and then conveying them into a life of perpetual apprenticeship of Jesus (Eph 4:13). This is an inside out conversion as the human will surrenders to the will of the Spirit (Rom 8), interacting in the context of the human heart. Consequently, being born again is the process of re-forming into the original image and orientation in which humans were created. In this way, humans put themselves back in the co-caretaker saddle, with God expanding his will on earth as in heaven through the individual human experience and expressed in the context of humanity as a force of godly influence. In this holistic, inside-out wholeness, where life is soul and soul is life, soul health can be understood as a form of holiness, or wholeness, where what is on the inside is what is on the outside. A living truth, *alētheia* in the Greek—truth that sets one free, as Jesus said it would.[10] This kind of congruent living frees one from hypocrisy. The flow of inside-out living is operationalized truth and only comes from a soul being reintegrated into its original design.

To the application of this salvation and sanctification theology to a very pointed and personal level, all salvation, sanctification, soul health, and spiritual warfare originate in the human heart. It's all an inside-out work. Consider this scenario from my ministry experience. For several

10. *Thayer's Greek Lexicon.*

years, an elder of mine would find me after each Sunday service to help me improve my sermon. He offered Bible passages that I overlooked, had better illustrations, would have made the application stronger, and would have made the appeal for response more pointed. I found myself preparing and delivering more to him each Sunday as if he were the only one there. Maybe it's testosterone, but it was a competition.

However, as I've found to be true in all conflicts or offenses, the problem was not *that* guy; it was *this* guy. The problem was not out there, but in here, in my heart. Every external stress, offense, conflict, or upsetting circumstance is more a revelation about my character rather than their character. The bottom line of soul health, and a basic psychological principle, is that no one can make you feel or think anything. You own you. This principle of soul ownership is why Jesus remained impervious to Pilate's threats, despite his ostensible power. Pilate pounded his chest and attempted to shake Jesus to the core with his death threat. But Jesus, living from the inside out, from a place of peace and security, trusting God's will as his will, said, "You haven't a shred of authority over me except what has been given you from heaven."[11] Jesus nodded to Pilate's political position God had put him in, but that was it. Jesus declared that Pilate's position was the extent of power. Jesus had all the real power. A power anchored in his identity as God's son, in whom God was well pleased.

God had not given that elder power over me to be insecure or offended. As a child of God, I am in the safest place I can be in the universe. If I'm angry, I choose to be. If I'm offended, threatened, or hurt, it's because I decided to be. Establishing a soul health life of increasing integration reorients our life from the inside out. May the river of life spring up, oh well, flowing out of me and you. Every external challenge is an opportunity for you to strengthen this inside-out flow. Don't give your security, peace, or power to anyone or anything. The only appropriate authority is the Spirit, and the Spirit of security, peace, and power flows from the inside out. Yes, "For God has not given us a spirit of fear and timidity, but of power, love, and self-discipline" (2 Tim 1:7).

No one aspect of this directional flow will amount to comprehensive soul health. For instance, working on how we think without recognizing the role of the will is chasing after the wind. Only a holistic vision of soul health integration, training into it and nurturing it, combined with the means to do so, will amount to soul health as intended by the original

---

11. John 19:11, paraphrased.

design and redemptive sanctification. Yes, this is an ode to Dallas Willard's VIM apprenticeship model.[12]

I'm sure the reader can imagine the impact the church could have if each person of God embraced and experienced this soul flow as the collective people of God. Imagine embracing and experiencing this soulful flow of peace and joy, and its impact on your marriage, family, friends, church, community, county, country, and the world. Yes, that's the **What** of general soul health. But what of the minister? Let's track back.

The minister is invited to adopt this holistic, inside-out approach to soul flow as a model for God's people, embracing comprehensive soul health. This ministerial modeling is similar to Paul's idea of imitating or following him as he imitates and follows Christ (1 Cor 11:1, Eph 5:1). This life modeling is for the soul health of the minister, then their family, and their church. A fundamental truth regarding this minister's modeling in the ministry is that a minister can't lead members to places they don't live. If a minister seeks the kingdom of the world, they cannot lead to the kingdom of God; they can only lead to where they live.

Here, we encounter our old nemesis: disoriented metrics. Our current problem is that the Western consumer mentality has infected the minister's soul. Many ministers imagine it will only be well with their souls if their church grows, so they can go full-time or get a promotion, popularity, etc. Yet this is misdirection by nefarious forces, worldly forces, or enticing external forces, inviting the minister to surrender to the kingdom of the world's metrics of soul dissatisfaction rather than the kingdom of God's metrics of soul satisfaction (Jas 1:14).

The bottom line is that a minister's soul cannot be made healthy by church growth, ministerial popularity, or increased funding. When we look to anything other than Christ to satisfy our souls, we're looking in all the wrong places. These external conditions and circumstances cannot produce health from the outside. As a professional minister, I spent way too much time suffering from the "if I can only just" syndrome. We often say to ourselves, if I can only just win this person to Christ. If I can just break the 75, 150, 300, etc. barrier, then I'd be OK and things would be easier, more effective, and productive. If I can only just _____. This modern ministry syndrome is chasing wind and attempting to gain the whole world of ministry at the expense of our souls. The only "soul-u-tion" is for the

---

12. Willard, *Renovation of the Heart*, 85.

The Uniqueness and Danger of Ministry

minister to repent and change the soul direction from an outside-in flow to an inside-out flow. But how?

We've explored the *Why* of ministerial soul health. Furthermore, I've attempted to show that the *What* of ministerial soul health can only be experienced from the inside out. With the foundation of a *Why* and *What* laid, we now focus on the *Work* of ministerial soul health.

3

The *Work* of Ministerial Soul Health

Stop trying to achieve soul health, and start training for it. Discipleship is never a matter of trying, but it is a matter of training.

THE KEY TO SOUL health for the Christian, specifically for the minister, is training over trying. Let me offer two intuitive examples of how trying is ineffective. Imagine someone who has never played baseball being included in a Major League Baseball home run derby. Now imagine a former home run derby winner telling, even yelling, at the first-time baseball player to try harder, and they will be able to hit a home run. Insane, right? The only sane approach for the first-time baseball player to hit a home run is to train for it.

Imagine another scenario of piano playing. I took piano lessons for a minute once. My fourth-grade female infatuation of the moment played the piano proficiently, and I wanted to play the piano as proficiently as she did. Therefore, I begged my mother incessantly for a piano and lessons. When I realized that just trying harder to play the piano would not instantly get me what I wanted, but training was the long and only route to piano proficiency, it became apparent that switching the focus of my female infatuation would be easier than playing piano. Of course, the only sane approach to playing the piano proficiently is to train for it. And, of course, the only rational approach to soul health is to train for it.

The Uniqueness and Danger of Ministry

There is no quick method to get soul health. One cannot hurry up and become Christlike. Soul health is only achieved by a long obedience in the same direction, as Eugene Peterson so aptly explains in his classic book of the same name.[1] This long obedience is often unwelcome in a culture of "get rich quick" schemes, fast food, next-day shipping, and instant coffee. Even as a minister, I am tempted by conferences and books that claim methods to attain spiritual and church health quickly. But if I'm honest about my temptation, it is always tied to wanting quick soul success through church growth or ministry prominence. Perhaps, like you, this path to soul health takes continual repentance and redirection. The repentance I am writing about is redirecting myself from the shallow to the deep, from the quick to the long, from trying to training. It's the only way.

Let's entertain the theory of soul health training, where repetition is the key. A common phrase in neuroscience originates from the vast amount of recent supportive research on Hebbian learning theory, characterized by the phrase "neurons that fire together, wire together."[2] The basic idea of psychologist Donald Hebb was that repetitive activity in a neural pathway results in strong behavioral tendencies, like language formation in early childhood.[3] Extrapolation of this theory has been applied to various aspects of human learning, emphasizing training over trying, such as hitting a baseball and playing the piano. Repetition strengthens the neural pathways of mental memory and muscle memory. Typing is a clear example. I'm typing this text without concentrating on where the letters are on the keyboard. This simple typing skill was only acquired by committing to a long obedience in the same direction. In other words, applied to soul health, only intentional repetition of soul health practice, like practicing piano, will reform our deformed souls increasingly into their original design. Let's dig deeper.

Consider human habit formation. Most of our daily behaviors are habits developed by repetition.[4] Coffee making, teeth brushing, driving a car, the sequence of bathing, and dressing are all examples of habits that have become deeply ingrained through repetition. At a minimum, creating a fragile habit routine takes about sixty days of consistent practice.[5] And far longer repetition if the habit is to become deeply formed in the person.

1. Peterson, *Long Obedience*.
2. Del Giudice, "Programmed to Learn?"
3. Milner, "Brief History."
4. Gardner, "Habit Formation and Behavioral Change."
5. Keller, "Habit Formation."

Imagine this repetitive habit-forming practice applied to our learned responses, such as anger, compassion, anxiety, generosity, fear, patience, lust, overeating, or comfort eating. We often consider these responses simply a matter of our nature or DNA, yet they're learned like a good or bad golf swing. As we saw with Hebbian learning theory, science is replete with evidence concerning the role of repetition in habit formation, as observed in behavior, organizational psychology, and neuroscience.

Dr. Deborah Ancona, a professor of management and organizational studies at MIT, states, "It turns out that we, as human beings, develop neural pathways, and the more we use those neural pathways over years and years and years, they become very stuck and deeply embedded, moving into deeper portions of the brain."[6] In the same article, neuroscientist Tara Swart acknowledges that focused attention and repetition are the primary means by which neural pathways can lead to habits or default behaviors.[7] It's intuitive that neural repetition results in deep behaviors or habits, such as driving a car, typing, playing the piano, riding a bike, or responses to anger, rejection, or sex. Can soul training reform or transform these already deeply ingrained habits into Christlikeness?

Dr. Andrew Newberg offers some insight in his groundbreaking book *How God Changes Your Brain*:

> In fact, the more a person thinks about God, the more complex and imaginative the concept becomes, taking on unique nuances of meaning that differ from one individual to the next. If you practice contemplation of God long enough, something surprising happens in the brain. Neural functioning begins to change. Different circuits become activated, while others become deactivated. New dendrites are formed, new synaptic connections are made, and the brain becomes more sensitive to subtle realms of (soul) experience.[8]

Going further, Dr. Curt Thompson, in his book *The Anatomy of the Soul: Surprising Connections Between Neuroscience and Spiritual Practices that Can Transform Your Life and Relationships*, explains that even though neuroplasticity becomes more intractable as we age, intentionally and regularly employing spiritual disciplines or exercises can abandon negative neural pathways for the creation of new positive neural pathways.[9]

---

6. Giang, "What It Takes," 4.
7. Giang, "What It Takes."
8. Newberg, *How God Changes Your Brain*, 3.
9. Thompson, *Anatomy of the Soul*, 46.

The point of surveying the theory of habit formation and the role of repetition is this: if a non-Christian can leverage their natural capacity to form deep, healthy habits without the Spirit, imagine what a Christian can do when they pair the effort of habit-forming repetition with the supernatural Spirit. Oh my!

This supernatural theory of Spirit-empowered repetition is not new information. I recall the apostle Paul's admonition to Timothy in 1 Tim 4:7, "Do not waste time arguing over godless ideas and old wives' tales. Instead, train yourself to be godly. Physical training is good, but training for godliness is far better, promising benefits in this life and the life to come."

Consider Phil 2:12–13: "Work hard to show the results of your salvation, obeying God with deep reverence and fear. For God is working in you, giving you the desire and the power to do what pleases him." In this passage, we have a toggle of work. We work, and God works. In God's grace, we put in the effort of living out our salvation, practicing the way of Jesus, and I mean, repetitiously practicing. This work is not for salvation but an effort to work out, to express, and experience our salvation. In his seminal book *The Great Omission*, Dallas Willard stated, "Grace is opposed to earning, not to effort. And it is a well-directed, decisive, and sustained effort that is the key to the keys of the Kingdom and to the life of restful power in ministry and life that those keys open to us."[10]

Yes, we work intentionally and regularly; however, God also works. He works in us, giving us the desire and power to do what pleases him. Hallelujah, our Christlikeness is not on us but on him. What a relief! The desire and the power are all generated by the Holy Spirit. We put in our effort to work on soul health, practicing repetitive soul exercises, and God affects the transformation. Slowly but surely. What a dream to break the negative shame loop of quick fixes and trying harder, and instead start a slow, longitudinal investment effort in simple, repetitive exercises that deeply form habits of soul health and hygiene. Does it sound a bit like a retirement investment pitch?

Yes, I'm sure you have a retirement dream. Slowly and incrementally, you invest faith and money in the economic miracle called compound interest. You have faith that one day, after a long, obedient financial investment routine in the same direction, compound interest will secure your financial wealth and security. Why not place similar faith in the miracle of compound soul health interest? Yes, long obedience toward soul health will ultimately

---

10. Willard, *Great Omission*, 34.

make your soul rich, where you naturally live as Jesus would if Jesus were you. This training is the goal of soul health, a natural default Christlikeness. It's what the science researchers of human nature we looked at earlier call "automaticity."[11] This automatic Christlikeness only comes from cultivating consistent soul health investment over time. Let's take a look at the visual representation of the compounding soul health interest miracle.

First, let's look at the common understanding of compounded financial interest. You can see in the graph that follows the contrast between simple interest, like a savings account, and compound interest, like an annuity or IRA. After intentionally investing small amounts of money in a compound interest account over a long period, the star on the graph represents a remarkable achievement. The economic theory of compound interest posits that a critical mass occurs within the investment vehicle, where the balance compounds on itself, accelerating the exponential growth and dramatically increasing wealth even with continuing small investments. The resulting wealth is the miracle of natural economic compound interest.

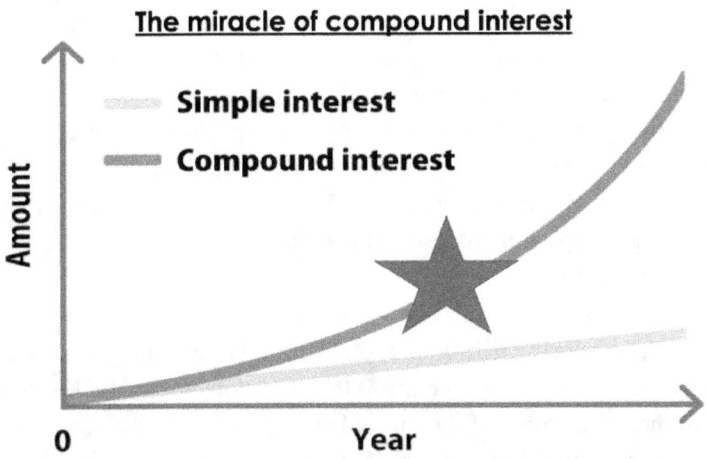

Now, let's overlay this compound interest understanding with the health of a human soul supernaturally infused with the Holy Spirit.

---

11. Keller, "Habit Formation."

The Uniqueness and Danger of Ministry

The vertical axis in the graph represents the goal of increasing Christlikeness, and the horizontal axis represents the passage of time. As we examine these evolving graphs, please note that the time axis represents a long, long time. I have no definitive time in mind; it's just a long time.

The flat red line in the slide above represents the quality of Christlikeness, correlated with regular soul health training exercises over a long time, such as fasting, prayer, study, silence, and worship. The reader must remember that there is typically no way of speeding up the miracle of Christlike compound interest. In other words, a Christian can't become soul-rich any quicker by praying more intensely at the altar or participating in a church-wide fast once a year.

As a Pentecostal, I believe in spontaneous miracles that break into a person's life, producing deliverance, breakthrough, or healing that dramatically change a person. However, this is the exception, not the rule. More specifically, these miraculous spikes in soul quality are often related to a specific issue, such as cancer, bitterness, or addiction. For the typical Christian, as Paul described in 2 Cor 3:18 and 1 Thess 4:1, followers of Jesus are on an evolutionary path of sanctification toward becoming more and more like Jesus. Even more pointedly, Paul in Eph 4:11–15 identifies the work of apostles, prophets, evangelists, pastors, and teachers as creating a salubrious environment conducive to equipping the followers of Jesus with examples and investment strategies focused on becoming more and more Christlike.

By softening our focus while reading the New Testament, we see the longitudinal investment strategy that apprenticeship to Jesus is. Christians can't hurry up and become Christlike. God's speed is slow. Developing a soul rich in Christlikeness is a strategic, intentional, and consistent practice of making small soul investments over time, which, by God's grace, produces in us a humanness more akin to the Edenic vision of Gen 1 and 2.

I want to make this as plain as possible, barring the rare and atypical miracle in the moment. With the guidance of professional ministers, Christians are to develop and consistently implement a soul health investment plan, work that plan, and God promises to make them rich in Christlikeness. Once we begin the habit of consistent soul investment, control of the result is Christ's and Christ's alone. The glory of our transformation can never be attributed to our ingenuity or effort. Our salvation and sanctification are by God's grace alone. However, a paraphrase from Dallas Willard is helpful here again: that grace is opposed to earning, not effort[12]. Philippians 2:12–13 exhorts us to pair our working hard to show the results of our salvation, while at the same time trusting God's grace that is working in us to give us the desire and power to do all things that please him. We work hard to invest in Christlikeness with investment tools like prayer, silence, meditation, fasting, worship, and serving, and God produces the results.

Like economic compound interest growth, soul compound interest growth early on is equally imperceptible. In the graph above, that which seems to be filling in above the Soul Health Investment Routine line represents the increasing results of Christlikeness, which naturally begins to be

---

12. Willard, *Great Omission*, loc. 34.

The Uniqueness and Danger of Ministry

experienced and expressed. The results are generally imperceptible, which does not mean the Christian is doing anything wrong. The key is to continue investing in soul formation with exercises that, over time, produce a habitual Christlikeness. We will survey these soul exercises later in this chapter when soul health planning is addressed.

A common experience related to compounding soul health interest is when the investor realizes they are rich in soul. This experience often takes the form of a comment someone offers about the noticeable difference in the life of the soul investor. The comment will likely relate to some aspect of Christlike character, such as the automatic response of peace in the presence of a stressful event. Or a comment about how the investor no longer appears consumed with popularity or church growth, but instead seems to be flowing in joyful ministry, regardless of the results. Perhaps the most robust evidence of a soul investor growing rich in Christlikeness emerges when a family member remarks about a positive change in personality, attitude, or behavior.

Finally, the slide below represents the miracle of soul health compound interest where the investor is experiencing and expressing what it is like to arrive by God's grace at a place where the investor is living up to the full standard of Christ in many areas of life (Eph 4:13). This fullness of Christ results in the non-anxious peace that passes all earthly understanding. What a beautiful dream for ministers to embrace and engage in themselves, as they lead their members to a place of Christlikeness where they live. Remember, you can't lead somewhere confidently that you don't live.

Get this: "When an initially goal-directed behavior becomes habitual, action initiation transfers from conscious motivational processes to context-cued impulse-driven mechanisms."[13] In other words, cultivating soul health is challenging until there's a breakthrough where our soul becomes automated to live like Jesus, actually and holistically. It's the miracle of compound soul health interest. Listen to the following biblical progression.

"It is no longer I who live but Christ who lives in me" (Gal 2:20). "This is the secret, Christ lives in you" (Col 1:27). "And the Lord—who is the Spirit makes us more and more like him as we are changed into his glorious image" (2 Cor 3:18). "Oh, my dear children! I feel as if I'm going through labor pains for you again, and they will continue until Christ is fully developed in your lives" (Gal 4:19). "So, we will be mature in the Lord, measuring up to the full and complete standard of Christ. Then we will no longer be immature like children" (Eph 4:13–14).

Eventually, this long obedience in the same direction yields the goal of all Christian faith and ministry—Christlikeness! We decrease, and Jesus increases so that we live naturally as if Jesus were us. But be sure, Godspeed is slow!

This long and slow process of soul health formation is not sexy (translation: attractive) in a consumer culture that worships short and fast methods. Resistance to such a slow and often tedious process will be met in you and those you minister to. As I stated, you can't lead somewhere you don't live. If you live in the fast and furious culture of quick fixes and short attention spans, you will lead the people of God in the same way. However, I'm offering what I believe is a better way: the way of the original creation, the way of Jesus and Paul, the way of the desert fathers and mothers of the church, the way of all God's soul-healthy people you recognize in your life. I'm confident that those people were people of slow and steady faithfulness to the way of Jesus.

May we not succumb to what Eugene Peterson calls the "tourist mindset" of religion: "There is a great market for religious experience in our world; there is little enthusiasm for the patient acquisition of virtue, little inclination to sign up for a long apprenticeship in holiness. Religion in our time has been captured by the tourist mindset."[14] We must live where we lead.

There is no doubt that God can indeed plow miracles of new neural pathways during an altar call. However, he's more likely to show you the

---

13. Gardner, "Habit Formation."
14. Peterson, *Long Obedience*, loc. 205.

The Uniqueness and Danger of Ministry

plow and ask you to put your hands on it. Continue to plow in a new neural direction with consistent soul health investments, and God will produce a bountiful crop of rich Christlikeness in your soul and those you minister to. In other words, get a plan and work the plan. No one gets lucky with soul health. So, partner with our planning God, get a soul health plan, and work the plan.

God is a planning God. Consider Jer 29:11: "'For I know the plans I have for you,' says the Lord. 'They are plans for good and not for disaster, to give you a future and a hope.'" Furthermore, consider Paul's assessment of God's planning nature in Eph 1:4–11:

> Even before he made the world, God loved us and chose us in Christ to be holy and without fault in his eyes. God decided in advance to adopt us into his own family by bringing us to himself through Jesus Christ. This is what he wanted to do, and it gave him great pleasure. God has now revealed to us his mysterious will regarding Christ, which is to fulfill his own good plan. And this is the plan: At the right time, he will bring everything together under the authority of Christ—everything in heaven and on earth. Furthermore, because we are united with Christ, we have received an inheritance from God, for he chose us in advance, and he makes everything work out according to his plan.

I'm not sure I can elaborate very much on these passages. The God of the Bible is a planning God. We were created in God's image, and as such, we can expect planning to be a part of our soul health.

God is also a partnering God. God invited humans to a partnership even before we ruined the world by surrendering our will to an inappropriate authority. Genesis 1:28, "God blessed them and said, 'Be fruitful and multiply. Fill the earth and govern it. Reign over the fish in the sea, the birds in the sky, and all the animals that scurry along the ground.'" This verse conveys our original mandate to partner with God in caretaking the world. Wow, God wants us as partners. Just because we are post Gen 3 does not change God's interest in having us as partners. As we saw earlier from Dallas Willard, God's grace is not opposed to effort but to earning. Therefore, God continues to invite us into partnership regarding our soul health, ultimately leading us again to a partnership of caring for the world.

One more time, let's look at Phil 2:12-13: "You *work hard* to show the results of your salvation, obeying God with deep reverence and fear. For *God is working* in you, giving you the desire and the power to do what pleases him" (emphasis added). He works, we work, he works, we work, we work, he works, and this toggling continues until that great day when God decides to set all things to rights.

> The bottom line here is that if you fail to plan for your soul, you plan to fail your soul.

General Soul Health Planning

I spent most of my Christian life living without a plan for my soul. I spent most of my ministry trying to lead God's people somewhere I'd never been and didn't live. It was indeed the blind leading the blind in soul health and formation. This understanding of soul formation was not a part of my early faith development or ministerial training. I entered ministerial training at the beginning of the tactical church growth movement in the late seventies and early eighties. According to this church growth preoccupation, all my success as a pastor would be due to consistently increasing the kingdom of the world's ABC metrics of attendance, buildings, and cash. I was chasing after the wind, leading others to chase it with me. If you've got a similar story, shake yourself, get a coffee, do some jumping jacks to wake up, and closely follow what comes next. Don't rush this part. The rest of this chapter is an invitation to stockpile practices that, when factored into an overall soul health plan, will have profound compound soul health interest over time. If you want to be soul-rich, you're gonna have to slow down, get a soul health plan, and work the plan. Then, and only then, help others curate their soul health plan and create a culture that encourages and holds all investors accountable for their soul health.

Here is a little story to begin this section. I'm a very competitive person with a high level of intensity when it comes to the sports I play. One of those sports is surfing. Thirty-five years ago, I was surfing a Newport Beach, California, break. The spot is dominated by entitled local surfers who dislike non-local surfers, thereby reducing their wave count. One of these locals started cussing my friend and me about us getting waves. We were both quickly enraged and got into a deep-water fight with the guy. It was ugly but not abnormal for me.

I surfed Hawaii's North Shore at a spot with locals a few years ago. As I rode down the line on the face of the wave, watching the beautiful coral reef and giant sea turtles pass under me, a local surf instructor pushed a student right out in front of me. I tried to turn, but my board hit the student, and a potential water brawl ensued. As the locals were cussing me and even threatened me with a punch, I responded in a peaceful, straightforward way that quickly de-escalated the moment. He capitulated to my peaceful response and paddled off, confused.

Reflecting on this experience, I was struck by how much my soul had matured to the point where I naturally responded as Jesus would have if Jesus were me. There was no need for me to fight the situation; I just needed an automatic response to float through the problem with peace. Sure, you could chalk this response up to being so much older or weaker, but have you ever seen an old guy get angry and ugly, even a Christian old guy, even a minister old guy? I have. I can only attribute this holistic soul transformation to the miracle of compound soul health interest—the basics of putting together a soul health investment plan.

As we begin with the practice of soul health planning, you'll need a few core practices to populate your soul health plan, which involves compounding Christlike interest. So, let's get very practical now and consider first soul renewal zones. These zones are rhythmic patterns of rest and renewal. The human circadian rhythm regulates the sleep-wake cycle. Consistent patterns or habits of sleep and waking times are crucial for maintaining physiological health and well-being.

Similarly, intentional patterns or habits of renewal beyond sleep significantly contribute to soul health. Remember that a holistic vision of the soul includes the human spirit/heart and the human mind, emotions, physical body, and social relationships. Therefore, developing a healthy rhythm of mental, emotional, physical, and social engagement and disengagement is as critical as attending any Bible study, prayer, or worship service. Consider incorporating the following renewal zones into your life for the sake of good soul health and hygiene.

Renewal Zones:

- Daily distraction
- Weekly diversion
- Quarterly disconnect
- Annual abandonment
- Triennial sabbatical

The Work of Ministerial Soul Health

Daily Distraction

- Any activity that distracts you from the regular stressors of typical life:
  - Wrestling with your children or grandchildren
  - Exercise that includes music or media unrelated to work/stress that you enjoy
  - Engagement of nature
  - Video game (measured by having a beginning and ending time)
  - Social media (measured by having a beginning and ending time)
  - Reading literature that is unrelated to work or life stress

Weekly Diversion

- A consistent activity that diverts you away from the heaviness and stress of your work-related responsibilities:
  - Sports participation—not passive watching, but active participation
  - Lunch with a friend unrelated to your work
  - Antiquing, yard sale-ing, museum, craft, or hobby engagement
  - Movie
  - Games with family or friends that are not stressful or related to work
  - Classes like yoga, spin, ceramics, foreign language, technology

  By the way, if you're having trouble thinking of people unrelated to your ministry context, you're suffering from the marginlessness of ministry.

Quarterly Disconnect:

- A multi-day retreat from ongoing stressful relationships and responsibilities that is renewing and refreshing.
  - Camping
  - Visiting family or friends
  - Visiting a historic site

- Festival
- Stay-cation where you hide yourself away in your house

Annual Abandonment

- At least a week-long experience where you plan to abandon ministry-related responsibilities, technology, and social media for the sake of silence and solitude:
  - Retreat center
  - Solo camping
  - Road trip
  - Immersive serving experience, i.e., missions trip, orphanage, inner-city shelter, etc.
  - Nature experience

Intentional planning and partnership with God in renewal zones is vital to soul health. Consider these renewal zone ideas as a starting point for crafting your soul health plan, incorporating renewal zones, and being creative.

The next renewal zone of the sabbatical will only be effective if the practice of the Sabbath is paired with it. I will address the Sabbath later in this chapter; however, for now, I know that the renewal zone of the sabbatical will be a rescue effort if it is not linked with regular Sabbath keeping. If, and only if, the sabbatical is related to regular Sabbath keeping, will the sabbatical be soul-renewing for the minister and not a rescue mission.

You'll notice that the sabbatical rhythm I'm proposing is three years. Many organizations have annual sabbaticals for ministry professionals, and many have five-year sabbatical rhythms, both of which are chosen for good reasons. Splitting the difference seems sensible here.

Although not listed in the graphic below, any sabbatical for less than three months misses the mark of a rich triennial sabbatical experience. Three months may seem fanciful to most people; however, a three-month sabbatical can be curated effectively in any context for a minister. A good spiritual director can easily help the minister create this three-month sanctuary experience in time. It doesn't matter if the full vocational or multi-vocational minister can conceive of a three-month sabbatical; it can be effectively curated with the proper help. For instance, imagine a bi-vocational minister.

Now imagine the minister and family taking a sabbatical every three years from ministry, permitting themselves to work their non-ministry job (perhaps planning a week-long retreat with vacation days) but not engaging in the work of ministry for three months. During these three months, with the help of church leadership and the regional office, they refrain from engaging in church business, preaching, teaching, or visiting the church campus. The minister on sabbatical follows the carefully curated sabbatical plan that does not include any professional ministry duties. Next, I will sketch a typical three-month sabbatical experience.

One month will be enough for the toxic pace and pressure of the ministry to abate. The first month of a well-curated sabbatical is a physiological detox of stress hormones, cortisol, and adrenaline. The chasing wind slowly stops. Eventually, our desperation to gain the whole world of ministry is gradually released from our soul grip. Anxiety will spike at first. Regret regarding the sabbatical commitment will haunt the first couple of weeks. Yet, by the end of the first month of detox, the minister will feel physically, mentally, and spiritually the decompression of the soul needed for the next two months.

During the second month of a triennial sabbatical, the minister will begin to experience the power of the relaxation response. Yes, the relaxation response is a thing. In my training as a psychotherapist, a unit on this phenomenon was phenomenally beneficial for me and my clients. The reality is that after a detox of oppressive stress hormones occurs during the first month, levels of the counterbalancing happy hormones dopamine and serotonin rise. At the same time, the minister's awareness of God's Spirit becomes unimpeded, and a fresh wind is felt in the soul. Creativity and a new capacity for perspective surge without the oppression of ministry pace and stress dampening it. The temptation during the second month will be to abandon the sabbatical when the minister feels the relaxation response kick in, and that would be a mistake. Let the rest settle down deep into the soul and have fun.

The third month is for turning attention to making decisions about how the minister will conduct themselves as a minister for their family and their church. The third month is a time to formalize the inspirations and revelations received during the first two months. As the soul renews, so will revelation and inspiration. During the third month, the challenge is not to think the minister is on sabbatical for the ministry. The minister is on sabbatical for the minister, and the minister alone. If the minister can only focus on personal inspiration and revelation, then the minister will be transformed during this third month. The following is an overview of a generic triennial sabbatical.

Triennial Sabbatical

- This sabbatical is:
  - not a vacation
  - authorized and supported by the church and regional leadership
  - strategic, involving only things that energize you and your family
  - soul formation-oriented
  - in consultation with a trusted soul coach
  - non-ministry-related in its goal(s), such as archery lessons, scuba certification, pottery course, etc.
  - a full family commitment
  - only involving rich and refreshing people

No one gets lucky with soul health because no one gets lucky with renewal zones. These zones don't just appear; they are planned and wrestled into existence. I say wrestled because that's what it feels like when planning and executing a renewal zone. Living with a rhythm of renewal directly opposes our cultural interests. To resist our consumer culture of 24/7 work and productivity addiction is a monumental challenge and can only be met with the supernatural force of the Spirit. Listen to biblical scholar Walter Brueggemann characterize our contemporary addiction to endless work, self-esteem validating productivity, and distraction: "The rat race of such predation and usurpation is a restlessness that issues inescapably in anxiety that is often at the edge of being unmanageable."[15] Brueggemann calls our fast and furious culture a predator. A predator, hmmm, reminds me of a Bible verse that no doubt you're also recalling right now: "Stay alert! Watch out for your great enemy, the devil. He prowls around like a roaring lion, looking for someone to devour. Stand firm against him, and be strong in your faith" (1 Pet 5:8–9).

---

15. Brueggemann, *Sabbath as Resistance*, loc. 124.

How our consumer culture roars. Our phones roar, our social media roars, our work roars, materialism roars, sports roar, news roars, politics roar, yet the still, small voice of the Spirit invites us to green pastures and quiet streams for renewal. Oh, how the Good Shepherd has prepared a table of holistic sustenance before us, yet we're too busy fighting the good fight to renew ourselves at his table. Gotta go, gotta run, really busy, you know—is often our life mantra. What would it be like for you to resist the rat race? What would it look like? Perhaps it would look like rhythms of renewal peppered throughout your schedule. Then, your life might resemble more of a reservoir than a pipeline. Lemme splain.

When offering counsel to young ministers, master minister Bernard of Clairvaux (1090–1153) shared this vision of the ministerial soul:

> The wise minister, therefore, will see their life as more like a reservoir than a pipeline. The pipeline simultaneously pours out what it receives; the reservoir retains the water until it is filled, then discharges the overflow without loss to itself. You, too, must learn to await this fullness before pouring out your gifts.[16]

Let's visually represent this wise notion for the ministerial soul.

Minister as a pipeline!
- Bernard of Clarivaux

I doubt Bernard had a waterslide in mind when counseling those young ministers, but this is what came to my mind. Are these vessels ever full? They are barely wet because they are constantly pouring out. For many

---

16. Foster, *Prayer*, 168.

The Uniqueness and Danger of Ministry

years in professional ministry, I believed that this was the only way to honor the self-sacrificing calling to professional ministry God had given me. As I said in the introduction, I quickly emptied myself and became a dry soul, hardly able to wring out a few drops of soul nurture here and there. That is, until the truth of Bernard's vision of a ministerial soul captured my imagination.

Here's a vision of what I believe Bernard was trying to convey.

My reality in professional ministry was that the needs of the people were always calling for more. This neediness fueled my need to be needed and tempted me to drain my soul dry, which I wholeheartedly did, to my demise. Now, I live and lead young ministers in much more of a Bernardian way, the way of the reservoir soul as a person and minister.

To make a gospel connection between Christ and Bernard's wisdom, I often find Jesus slipping away to renewal zones, where he could be alone. My favorite passage about Jesus and his propensity for renewal is Luke 5:15–16: "But despite Jesus' instructions, the report of his power spread even faster, and vast crowds came to hear him preach and to be healed of their diseases. But Jesus often withdrew to the wilderness for prayer."

Because Jesus poured out his gifts, his church grew, and when it did, he withdrew. This withdrawal is so counterintuitive to me. How did he imagine he'd be able to keep the crowds happy and coming if he frequently withdrew from the people that he was drawing? Doesn't Jesus understand what it means to maximize the social media algorithm? Seriously, demand requires supply; what was Jesus thinking?

And what about when he railroaded his ministry into a ditch right at the beginning, when, after his baptism, the voice of God spoke affirming words over him and came up out of the water as a superstar? The first thing he does is disappear. More accurately, what was the Spirit thinking? It was the Spirit that drove Jesus into the wilderness. Doesn't the Spirit know that he could have equally driven Jesus' career into the wilderness?

Bernard took his cue for training young ministers from a page out of Jesus' ministry playbook. Live as a reservoir, not a pipeline. This advice for a young minister is also suitable for parents, husbands, and humans.

It's a given that Jesus is a model for us to follow as ministers. Therefore, as we live like Jesus, we also lead others to live like him, or vice versa. Consequently, it's incumbent on the professional minister to encourage each of the people God has given them to shepherd to build and fill a reservoir of the soul. But how? Perhaps we should start with the nine commandments.

We live in a postmodern culture that is unacquainted with the nine commandments. Although they are chiseled in the walls of most public buildings in America, many people still don't know what they mean in the context of world history or their relevance to living today. You've surely preached sermons, taught classes, and facilitated small group studies on the nine commandments. The nine commandments provide the foundation of civilized morality and law. America and the West would not exist as they do today without the nine commandments.

Perhaps the Ten Commandments should be edited to nine, considering that very few Christians or Christian ministers take the fourth commandment seriously to keep the Sabbath holy. Here's how the Deuteronomy version reads:

> Observe the Sabbath day by keeping it holy, as the Lord your God has commanded you. You have six days each week for your ordinary work, but the seventh day is a Sabbath day of rest dedicated to the Lord your God. On that day, no one in your household may do any work. This includes you, your sons and daughters, your male and female servants, your oxen and donkeys, and other livestock, and any foreigners living among you. All your male and female servants must rest as you do. Remember that you were once slaves in Egypt, but the Lord your God brought you out with his strong hand and powerful arm. That is why the Lord your God has commanded you to rest on the Sabbath day. (5:12–15)

Sabbath

Attempt the following experiment if you're courageous enough. Announce to your spouse that you've uncovered a new truth: apparently, Christians can drop one of the Ten Commandments. So, you've decided to drop the seventh commandment prohibiting adultery. Announce to your spouse that you are free now to commit adultery whenever you want. Let me know how that conversation goes.

Recently, while covering this section of my ministerial soul health clinic, I asked how spouses would react to such a suggestion. One woman raised her hand and said, "That's fine, I'm going to stop keeping the sixth commandment, 'Thou shalt not murder!'" Her husband got the message.

I don't intend here to argue whether this command is a binding command or not. However, even if it is not exegetically a binding commandment, such as not lying or committing adultery, it was part of the code that founded the basis of most national laws. At the very least, it would be prudent to consider the wisdom of observing the Sabbath.

Consider the creation account in Genesis. First, we can agree that God didn't and doesn't need rest. God does not wear out or need a break from work. Yet, humans do. On the sixth day, God created humans in His image. Everything was very good. However, the first thing God commanded humans to do was rest. The seventh day, the first day of the week, was a day of rest. Humans don't rest from work; humans work from rest. Rest is the priority. Rest was the priority of God's kingdom and his kingdom caretakers. Before there were God's people, the Jews, there were just God's people of original creation, and God's original people were to prioritize rest before starting the other six days of work.

Listen to the wise interpretation of Wayne Muller from his excellent book *Sabbath: Finding Rest, Renewal, and Delight in Our Busy Lives*:

> The ancient rabbis teach that on the seventh day, God created *menuha*—tranquillity, serenity, peace, and repose—rest, in the deepest possible sense of fertile, healing stillness. Until the Sabbath, creation was unfinished. Only after the birth of *menuha*, only with tranquillity and rest, was the circle of creation made full and complete.[17]

I also love how the Sabbath in the Ten Commandments is linked to a celebration of freedom. The fourth command is the only command

---

17. Muller, *Sabbath*, 35.

referenced as a memorial of God's deliverance from bondage. Yet, we often bow to the current cultural pharaoh who reigns over our Western capitalistic consumerism, shaming us into busyness that consistently acculturates us to break the fourth commandment. The cry of consumerism's performance-based life philosophy, fueled by discontent, is "more bricks, more bricks, more bricks, more bricks." We're living in sin! This non-Sabbathing sin is not the way God intended us to live as humans.

Consider how Pete Scazzero puts it:

> Sadly, many of us remain under a harsh and controlling taskmaster, a "Pharaoh" who now lives inside our heads, telling us we can't stop or rest. The culture shackles us in chains, telling us that our only value is what we achieve or produce, and that we are losers unless we accomplish more, whatever the cost may be. We are doing well only if things are "bigger and better." We compare ourselves to other leaders who seem to produce more bricks more quickly, and we wonder, What's my problem?[18]

Old Testament scholar Walter Brueggemann recognizes our culture of consumerism as a form of soul predation:

> Endless predation so that we are a society of 24/7 multitasking to achieve, accomplish, perform, and possess. However, the demands of market ideology pertain as much to consumption as they do to production. Thus, the system of commodity requires that we want more, have more, own more, use more, eat more, and drink more. The rat race of such predation and usurpation is a restlessness that issues inescapably in anxiety that is often at the edge of being unmanageable.[19]

Once again, we see the predator prowling. Are you being devoured by a consuming culture? Resist the devil by Sabbathing. Of your seven days, commit one to just be with God. Recover the first Sabbath when the first human's full-day experience was to do nothing but hang out with God to enjoy his work of physical and human creation and bask in the "very good" of it all.

In the same way, celebrating the Fourth of July as Americans reminds us of our freedom from oppression; keeping the Sabbath holy is a weekly reminder of our freedom from the pharaoh of our oppressive, sinful nature. So, what if the command isn't technically binding? It's just brilliant.

---

18. Scazzero, *Emotionally Healthy Leader*, 158–59.
19. Brueggemann, *Sabbath as Resistance*, loc. 99.

Now, let's get back to being practical. When teaching on Sabbath as a soul health planning practice of top priority, I had a person in the audience push back during a time of taking questions who said, "I appreciate your emphasis on taking a day off, but the devil never takes a day off. What about that?" I replied, "Well, if you want to live like the devil, that's your prerogative. I, however, would rather live like Jesus." That story brings up a good point: taking a day off. Is Sabbath a day off? If so, a day off from what?

The Sabbath is not a day off in the traditional Western sense. Sabbath is a ceasing of all paid and unpaid work. Paid work is what you do for your vocation. Perhaps you get paid to do accounting, truck driving, childcare, ministry, or a combination of several vocations to make ends meet. Unpaid work includes tasks such as cutting grass, cleaning after the dog or children, washing clothes or dishes, shopping, and paying bills. Most folks take a day off from paid work to do all their unpaid work. This type of day off is not a Sabbath.

Sabbath is a weekly twenty-four-hour period for ceasing all paid and unpaid work for soul rest, recovery, and worship. Let that sink in. Imagine a whole day every week where you do nothing but satisfy your soul and flop down in God's presence for renewing rest. Now, imagine a corporate Sabbath where your church does nothing. Take a Xanax. Breathe. It's just an imagination exercise. Just imagine a personal and communal life like that.

In his classic book on the Sabbath, Abraham Heschel said that the Sabbath was a sanctuary in time for the whole community.[20] Sunday in the church sanctuary is, of course, an impossible Sabbath for a minister. So, what does a minister do?

Jesus offers freedom to curate our Sabbath as we see fit. Jesus removed the legalism of the Sabbath yet affirmed its wisdom. "Then Jesus said to them, 'The Sabbath was made to meet the needs of people, and not people to meet the requirements of the Sabbath'" (Mark 2:27). Be consistent and creative with your Sabbath, but not complacent!

If you can't conceive of a twenty-four-hour Sabbath, then conceive of a twelve-hour Sabbath, or eight, sixteen, thirty-six, whatever you can imagine, give it a try. Set yourself up for success, not failure. Often, we set our aim too high and miss the target altogether. Relax! Too many ministers consider the Sabbath as requiring adherence to a Judaic formula or a rigid discipline of spiritual exercises for twenty-four hours. Stop that! The Sabbath is about the joy of simply being with God and others; we are refreshed

20. Heschel, *Sabbath*, 38.

by doing only things that offer the Holy Spirit the opportunity to restore our souls, as indicated in Ps 23.

I'll offer my own Sabbath rhythm here as an example. When I was pastoring, my Sabbath began on Thursday sundown and lasted until Friday sundown. Typically, my wife and I would plan meals out or order in, so there was no food prep burden. Sometimes, I would grill because that's restorative to me. Thursday night was soccer night for me. I played competitive soccer in an over-thirty-five men's league with the same guys for many years. This physical testosterone-fest was fantastic for stress relief. It was not a church league. A church league would have defeated the purpose of restorative rest. I didn't want any of my church people around. The guys on my team respected my space. To those guys, I was not Pastor Steve; I was just Steve, who would even get red-carded at times without judgment. During halftime, I would visit the Salvadoran pupusa lady's cart and stock up for lunch on Friday.

Friday Sabbath would begin with a very slow morning, where marital romance often eased us into the day. How's that for a way to sell Sabbath to ministers? Moving on. Our phones and computers also observed the Sabbath. My wife and I celebrate the Sabbath differently in the morning. She is more spontaneous and free, often taking in morning talk shows or romantic comedies, while weaving in Bible reading and times of fluid prayer. I like silence and the ancient practices of *lectio* or *visio divina*. I'm a Pentecostal, and I use my tongue's prayer language as a form of contemplative prayer. This practice frees me from praying with my mind, setting my soul free to float. At some point, my wife and I circle back to each other for the sacred pupusa lunch meal. Then, after lunch, we often take a thrift or antique shop tour, perhaps visiting friends or family who don't drain us but fill our soul's reservoir. Sometimes, we venture to the beach where I'll surf, and she'll stroll. The day wraps with a meal out for dinner and some mutually pleasurable activity that doesn't drain but fills our soul reservoir.

For the ministry couple, avoiding the trap of talking ministry shop is crucial. As I'll address in the next chapter, ministers' spouses are uniquely engaged in ministry as deeply as the minister. Therefore, like non-ministry couples often default to discussing the kids, ministry couples often default to discussing the church. This shop talk must be avoided like poison ivy.

Here's a list for those who like a more linear approach to Sabbath.

The Five Ss of Sabbath

- *Supply*—in advance, supply the Sabbath with everything you need to make it rich and restful. This advanced supply enables you to secure groceries, wash clothes/dishes, plan for ticketed or reservation-oriented events, and maintain a clear schedule.

- *Stop*—cease all regular paid and unpaid work. Make this a hard stop. Just cut work off. Our consumer culture has misled us into believing that time is money. Therefore, we struggle with taking time to rest because we have a love or fear of money. In ministry, we struggle with the reality of nickels and noses. If we take time off to rest from the ministry, we will lose ground, attracting noses and, consequently, we won't receive their nickels. This anxiety is the shadow sin of ministry, striving to gain the whole world of ministry while losing our souls. In this capitulation to consumerism, we lead God's people into the same consumer quagmire in which we find ourselves.

- *Settle*—after the hard stop of work, front-load your Sabbath with exercises that allow you to settle all insecurities about work and trust God. It generally takes some time to detox on the Sabbath at the beginning. Figuring out some activity, exercise, recitation, or prayer to help you settle your soul is vital for a healthy Sabbath. Soccer was my way. I allowed myself to completely immerse myself in the activity and think about it afterward until I drifted off to sleep. Trust that God's got your back like he did the Israelites leaving Egypt. Work will chase you; don't look back.

- *Savor*—soak in beauty, joy, peace, love, and fun only. Savor only soul-nurturing things. Be mindful of your entertainment, reading, listening, gaming, and other activities. Make sure to savor beauty, joy, fun, peace, and more.

- *Synchronize*—recognize that seeking to gain the whole world of ministry will distance your soul from God, the giver of life. Repent and synchronize your heart with God's love, sovereignty, and providence. Craft a personalized worship experience that refreshes your relationship with God. Just because you work for God professionally does not mean you're close to God personally. Leverage some Sabbath practice to refresh your relationship with God.

As my Sabbath routine evolved, I realized I could adopt a micro-Sabbath approach daily. This micro-Sabbathing is akin to keeping renewal zones as I described above. Micro-Sabbathing is finding a quiet place to breathe deeply, re-centering all my scattered senses on the Holy Spirit within me. With each breath, I imagine receiving a type of soul resuscitation as I breathe in the life-giving Spirit and exhale carnal toxicity. Micro-Sabbathing is similar to keeping what many call the daily office, which creates sanctuary space in the quiet of your car just before you drive off, or in the restroom stall, behind the door of your office, or taking a walk to a deserted part of your workplace or home.

A story I heard about the mother of John and Charles Wesley, Susanna, is an excellent example of micro-Sabbath keeping. Susanna had many children, and her husband was often away on long trips, leaving her to manage the 24/7 work of the family and farm. The story is that several times a day, she would sit down in a chair, bring her apron up over her head to create enough space for a moment of soul-centering prayer. The story continues that the children were trained to be reverent of this micro-Sabbathing. Surely, she put the fear of God in them. The point is that intentional Sabbath and micro-Sabbath keeping are doable.

One professional consideration for ministers on the Sabbath: train your church by teaching on the Sabbath and then model it for them. First, start Sabbathing yourself. Second, educate your leadership about the Sabbath and require them to observe it. After modeling, teaching, and requiring your leadership to observe the Sabbath, teach on the Sabbath from the pulpit and lectern. Please inform your congregation that you will be unavailable from x time to x time each week.

Of course, emergencies are natural and may invade the minister's Sabbath from time to time. You'll have to navigate this nuance of ministerial Sabbath. The temptation will be to allow all so-called emergencies to invade your Sabbath. Be vigilant about keeping the Sabbath holy. Protect your Sabbath from the slow creep of ministry into your Sabbath. Remember, Sabbath is how you honor the reservoir soul principle. Put a proverbial fence around your Sabbath. As a local church minister for thirty-eight years, I would often move or skip my Sabbath to attend funerals, weddings, or vital church-wide events. However, these became fewer and fewer as I grew in Sabbath strength. Just say, "No! I'm on Sabbath and will only be available to God, not you."

Slowly, you, your family, and your church will acculturate as you engineer a culture that honors the Sabbath. My church caught on after a few years of living, teaching, and observing the Sabbath. Around 4:00 p.m. on Thursday, I would get bombarded with emails, texts, and phone calls, starting with, "Pastor, I know your Sabbath is about to start, but if I could . . . before you begin Sabbath." This Thursday afternoon routine became quite humorous to my wife and me.

It suffices to say, just do it—just Sabbath. Eventually, you'll develop the soul muscle memory for it, and the Sabbath will automatically benefit you, your family, and your church. Some notable authors have written extensively on Sabbath practice, including Ruth Haley Barton, Walter Brueggemann, Richard Foster, Dallas Willard, Wayne Muller, and Marva J. Dawn. And there is no better resource to help you help your church experience Sabbath than John Mark Comer's work with Practicing the Way.[21]

My Soul Health Planning

I'd like to introduce you to the ancient practice of soul health planning, also known as the *regula vitae* (rule of life) by the ancient church. The wording of the rule of life can evoke all kinds of unintended negative responses. First, the *regula vitae* or rule of life sounds archaic. Second, the word "rule" sounds like a command or law to which punishment may be attached. Because of this, I've chosen to reframe the early church practice as a soul health plan or SHP.

Doing this demystified the process for my church. I'm a spiritual formation dude and love Latin-sounding practices. *Regula vitae* sounds so much more spiritual than a soul health plan. However, Latin is not intuitive in our cultural moment and presents barriers that we want to avoid. Going forward, I'll be using the soul health plan language.

The following soul health planning is my design. I draw inspiration from a diverse range of sources, but ultimately, this is something I've designed for myself and the churches I've served, aiming for simplicity and accessibility. Soul health planning is not complicated or mystical.

I see a cooking recipe as a loose collection of suggestions. That's how I see soul health planning, as relaxed but not sloppy. Therefore, I have provided a soul health plan worksheet, SHP examples, and numerous resources to help you build your SHP in appendix 2. After reviewing the following

---

21. www.practicingtheway.org.

section, enjoy the appendix as you partner with the Holy Spirit to create your soul health plan.

I referenced Dallas Willard's brilliant insight: "Grace is opposed to earning, not to effort."[22] None of what I'm about to offer concerns earning God's grace; quite the opposite. The remainder of this chapter focuses on our efforts to promote soul health training, powered by God's grace. God can leverage our soul health training effort to do in us what we cannot do in ourselves, namely, transform us into the image of Christ.

Let's break down soul health planning into an annual practice. First, invite the Holy Spirit to inspire you with a soul health goal related to the year. Set aside time with the Holy Spirit to recognize God's presence and invite the Holy Spirit to inspire you with a vision of what God wants for your soul in the upcoming year. Then boil that big vision down into a brief sentence or two that summarizes the Holy Spirit's big idea for your soul in the upcoming year.

A common impediment to soul goals for ministers is the misconception that their soul goal is directly related to their ministry context. Many ministers struggle to engage in spiritual exercises without making them all about the ministry rather than the minister. Come to the Holy Spirit like a Christian, not clergy. Take the meditation posture only as a child of God. Relax, don't put pressure on yourself to discern your soul's goal. Simply invite the Holy Spirit to begin the proprietary inspirational process that only you and the Holy Spirit enjoy.

Here are some of my past soul goals:

- To cultivate a non-anxious, unselfconscious presence where people feel refreshed in my presence.
- To live light and love heavy, embodying a peaceful and joyous personality that creates restful space for others.
- To live an increasingly open life to God, self, and others.
- To assert in my daily walking around life the principles of spiritual formation I've learned and am learning from those soul guides I trust. To live consistently from the center, reconciling the physical and spiritual in thought and deed.

---

22. Willard, *Renovation of the Heart*, 85.

- To thoroughly detach my soul from every attachment that serves as an impediment to Christlike character. It will be the year of detachment.
- To have more fun.

A soul goal cannot be right or wrong. It's your soul goal, no judgment.

Next is the soul word. This soul word emerges from the soul's goal. It may be a word inside or outside the soul's goal. It's a word that embodies the soul's goal. It's a word that you can breathe as prayer. A word you breathe at any time during your day, as a prayer that centers you consistently and calls you back to your soul's goal. Ask the Holy Spirit to give you one word to anchor your soul's goal. Make it one syllable if possible. One-syllable words are easy to breathe as prayer. On rare occasions, I've adopted multi-syllable soul words.

Here are some of my past soul words:

- Love
- Repent
- Light
- Peace
- Reveal
- Open
- Legacy

A soul word cannot be right or wrong. It's your soul word, no judgment.

The next element of a reasonable soul health plan is a collection of soul training exercises. Soul exercises refer to the classic notion of spiritual disciplines. However, I reframed *regula vitae* as a soul health plan for the same reason. I've exchanged the language of spiritual disciplines with soul exercises. This word choice exchange also fits better in the context of a soul health plan; exercising is simply intuitive in any health-related plan.

When developing a plan for soul exercise, consider your soul goal and identify exercises that will help you achieve it. This soul exercise selection process is similar to creating a physical health plan. If the goal of a physical health plan is to lose weight, then fat-burning exercises like walking, running, biking, or swimming would be employed. If the goal of the physical health plan is to bulk up, then muscle-building exercises, such as weight lifting, would be used. Think of these soul health exercises in terms of daily, weekly, monthly, quarterly, or annual frequency. You don't need all frequencies in each section, but you can.

Depending on the soul's goal, exercises such as fasting, Bible memorization, meditation, silence, worship, prayers of awakening, and examen may be employed. For instance, imagine an evangelistic soul goal. Then, exercises such as memorizing evangelistic passages, studying Gospel passages, committing to an evangelism outreach, and curating your salvation story would be beneficial.

Imagine a soul goal that embodies the theme of peace. Then, soul exercises like silence, solitude, memorizing Bible passages on peace, studying Bible passages on peace, and memorizing Ps 23 as a breath prayer. Many more exercises are provided in the appendix.

Here are some of my past soul exercises (explanations are included in appendix 2):

- *Daily*:
  - Prayer of awaken to non-attachment and pre-sleep examen prayer of attachments from the day.
  - Set a few daily phone reminders to take every thought captive to the obedience of Christ.
  - To practice soul-seeing and feeling through the eyes and heart of Jesus. It is an exercise to soften my soul focus to see and think about those around me more like Jesus sees and thinks about them.
- *Weekly*:
  - Guard my Sabbath as resistance to attachment.
  - Practice random "soul staring" to see God everywhere. This exercise will increase awareness of God's presence outside the sanctuary.
  - Post sticky notes along my daily path to remind me that God is with me.
  - Practice not having to have the last word or win an argument or discussion.

- Increase Bible reading volume for purely personal reasons as opposed to professional reasons.
- Sabbath (every SHP must have Sabbath as a weekly exercise).

- *Monthly*:
  - Maintain secrecy.
  - Fast—for at least one day, I abstain from solid food and drink only water, skipping breakfast and lunch. This way, hunger serves as a reminder of the traits I want the Holy Spirit to transform.
  - Exercise the spiritual fruit of gratitude. Formally, I thank someone for the contribution they made to my life.

- *Annually*:
  - Spend three days in silence and solitude.
  - Spend one day visiting the National Museum of Art in silence and solitude.
  - Spend one day at the beach working hard not to work.
  - Take a three-day retreat from all electronic engagement to be with God in real time.

A soul exercise cannot be right or wrong. It's your soul exercise, no judgment.

The next element of soul health planning is personal practices. Again, consider these practices in terms of daily, weekly, monthly, quarterly, and annual cycles. Also, like soul exercises, personal practices are often linked to the soul's goal. These personal practices are frequently confused with soul exercises but are critically different. Where soul exercises are easily generalizable to any Christian, personal practices are unique to the individual. Any Christian can choose to spend time in silence and solitude or fast as a general spiritual exercise. However, not every Christian would consider playing a game with their spouse or cutting meal portions in half as a generic soul exercise, which is why there is a need for individualized personal practices distinct from soul exercises. Playing a game with your spouse or cutting meal portions in half are examples of personal practices tailored to your soul by the Holy Spirit.

The Holy Spirit tailors personal practices to each individual. Take me, for instance. I grew up in a very dissonant and often unaffectionate environment. So, physical and verbal affection were not natural outworkings of my personhood. Therefore, while pondering my next SHP, the Holy Spirit brought to my attention the following personal practice: I will physically touch and verbally express love to my immediate family. This practice was fleshed out to mean touching a family member while saying "I love you." This practice was highly individualized, tailored to address something the Holy Spirit wanted to correct in my past.

You have a unique life experience that the Holy Spirit will use to inspire specific practices tailored just for you. Here, you invite the Spirit to divide soul and spirit, joint and marrow, exposing every thought and desire.

I would lead my elders through the SHP process each year and schedule time to review it early in the new year. At one such review, one of my elders shared that while meditating in silence for the Holy Spirit to help him create this new SHP, the Spirit inspired him to give up sexual intimacy with his wife for the Lenten season. He said that the Spirit revealed to him that his sexual formation needed reform and that fasting from sex was the way to get at it. His wife reluctantly agreed, and they entered Lent. Their post-Lent self-report was that midway through Lent, they both experienced unique breakthroughs regarding their sexuality, healing, and maturity, and their sexual life was changed for the better.

Here are some of my past personal practices:

- *Daily*:
  - I will wake each morning determined to live a life without guile. I will do this by conditioning myself to remember daily that no guile was found in Nathaniel, and I want none found in me.
  - I will pray the prayer of examen at bedtime, allowing the Holy Spirit to scrutinize my life for guile specifically.
  - I will thank God for someone I don't like and confess that God's thoughts and feelings for them are the same as God thinks and feels about me.
  - I will wake each morning with the determination to take every thought captive to the obedience of Christ so that my negative personality traits may be transformed.

The Uniqueness and Danger of Ministry

- I will physically touch my wife and family as I breathe a prayer for me to see them as you see them.
- Work on memorizing Ps 42 as a new breath prayer to help my soul embrace suffering with hope.
- Ruthlessly eradicate all negative, cynical, specious, draining people, thought patterns, behaviors, and circumstances from my life.

- *Weekly*:
  - Play a board/card game with my wife and/or friends.
  - I will ask a close friend or family member to point out any potential evidence of guile within me.
  - Become increasingly more interested in new experiences and people.
  - Become hypervigilant to opportunities for openness.
  - On Sabbath, I will call each of my children just to chat.
  - Refuse to get caught up in bemoaning the aging process and challenge all who bemoan it to reframe aging as a spiritual discipline of soul formation, not debilitating drudgery.
  - Engage in anti-attachment behaviors, such as being generous with money, watching HGTV despite personal preferences, and embracing criticism without anxiety.

- *Monthly*:
  - Directly yet kindly challenge someone negative, cynical, specious, or draining to repent.
  - Memorize a new short Bible passage or Christian prayer to reform my mind.
  - Engage a counselor to process good mental health and hygiene.

- *Quarterly*:
  - Take a short trip with LaDon only, somewhere we've never been but have always wanted to check out.
  - Taking a two-day break with LaDon and friends for rest and relaxation.
  - Read a book of fiction for fun.

The Work of Ministerial Soul Health

- *Annually*:
    - Take a long trip with LaDon, somewhere we've never been but have always wanted to explore.
    - Visit the National Museum of Art for a day of reflection.
    - Write my family letters of reflection regarding myself as a spouse and father.
    - Spend a week at a center on a guided retreat.
    - Write something for publishing.

A personal practice cannot be right or wrong. It's your practice, no judgment.

Soul health planning is an intensely individual practice; however, it can also be healthy for a family and church. Eventually, consider inviting your spouse into the SHP process. Then, expand that invitation to your immediate and perhaps extended family. This past year, I had the unique experience of having all my family, including my son and daughter-in-law, with me. I asked the family to craft an SHP beforehand to share during the New Year's holiday. What a sweet joy to share what the Holy Spirit has inspired and revealed to each of us about the health of our souls. With all that experience, you may be interested in making soul health planning an annual church family experience.

I expected my ministry staff and top church leadership to create a new SHP each year. Additionally, I invited the entire church to participate in the SHP process. Like Sabbath, I began with modeling and then teaching. Each fall, I would pick a Sunday to address our annual SHP practice with the congregation. Everyone was emailed the same information I've provided for you in appendix 2.

In January each year, I would share my SHP with the church as an example. This practice also gave me accountability, as many of those who attended would check on me about my soul health throughout the year. A standard part of SHP follow-up would occur quarterly in church leadership meetings and life groups. Life group leaders were instructed to have quarterly check-ins with their group, not as a matter of shaming but as encouragement and gentle accountability.

Caution: soul health planning is not a performance or competition. Relax. Don't overplan or underplan. Soul health is not about winning God's or anyone's approval. It's just about the long, slow, consistent, creative small investments made in your soul health account throughout your life. Remember, there are loads of Sabbath resources in appendix 2.

Covenantal Friendship

To expand the practical **Work** of soul health, do you have covenantal friendships? According to Barna research, relationships are a minister's weakest link in their soul health, and they don't know it.[23] It seems that many ministers and minister spouses assume that the quantity of relationships due to the ministry context suffices for relational satisfaction. However, relationships within the ministry context may supply extensive quantitative relationships, but they appear to lack qualitative sufficiency.

I asked Dr. Derwood Perkins, an executive in denominational leadership with a significant quantity of relationships, how his soul was doing. He remarked that in his many years of ministry experience and a large number of Christian relationships, no one had ever asked him that question as directly as I did. His experience had been my experience. In my thirty-eight years of ministry experience, until I trained my church to ask, I had also never been asked that question in the context of ministry. Pastors are intensely preoccupied with how the souls in their parish are doing. However, it's a rare parish that is preoccupied with how the soul of their pastor is doing. In professional ministry, pastors don't have a pastor. Even if their denominational leadership is tasked with pastoring pastors, it's just an impossible relationship due to the power and responsibility differential. I love the idea of pastoring of pastors, but it's simply unrealistic in general.

I'd like to think Paul David Tripp's idea of the pastor's church as a place of safe mutual pastoral relationships, but I just don't think it's realistic either.[24] An essential element of soul health for a minister is indeed an authentic covenantal community where they can be transparent and themselves, dropping the title pastor for just their name. It would be a rare pastoral context to find such a community. Therefore, this covenantal community needs to be sought outside the minister's church context, and perhaps even outside their larger denominational context. The key is that the minister and their spouse find such a community. I will go as far as to claim

---

23. Barna, *Relationships of Today's Pastors*, 13.
24. Tripp, *Dangerous Calling*, 83–96.

The Work of Ministerial Soul Health

that covenantal community must be found, or the minister and spouse will succumb to the uniqueness and danger of ministry.

To press the point, as a minister, it's tough to tell your church buddy about your struggle with porn and then get up and preach about sexual purity. Typically, you and they will eventually have a problem with that kind of relationship awareness. Think of it this way, once Jesus becomes Christ, it's impossible to see him anymore as just Jesus. In the same way, once Steve becomes Pastor Steve, it's impossible to see him anymore as anything but Pastor Steve. On the soccer pitch, in the grocery store, in a small group (whether leading or not), a little league field, anywhere, once the title "pastor" is given and received, it's as if the title is tattooed on the forehead. It's inescapable.

I know that narrative is not normative, so my story may not be your story. However, to illustrate what I think is an evidence-based point, I offer this curious story. I love soccer and played competitively in a local indoor "old man's" league for twenty years. I used my Thursday night soccer gig as the beginning of my Sabbath, which was every Friday. After a long week of ministry, I would give vent to my pent-up testosterone by playing soccer with non-church friends. I say non-church friends because I was craving a place where I was just Steve, not Pastor Steve. I desperately needed margin. So, one hot summer night in the Easy-Bake Oven of the Soccerdome, I was venting testosterone on the pitch and hacked this guy down on the other team. We both tumbled to the turf, where he bounced back up and ran to where I was cussing all the way. He grabbed the ball from another player, dropped it, and kicked it into my chest while I lay on the floor. One of his teammates ran up to him and said, and I quote, "Dude, you can't do that to him, he's a priest!" To which the offended player declared, "Oh, s___!" Turning his gaze to me, he bowed, crossing himself and begging, "Father, forgive me for I have sinned." I had been outed. My anonymity was gone. The following Thursday night when I arrived, several players greeted me with a sincere, "Hello, Father," or "Bless you, Padre."

So, where can a pastor turn to be themselves or share personal issues? Generally, nowhere. Safe spaces just don't seem to exist. Bottom line, for most pastors, having a rich network of trusted friends where raw transparency and accountability rule as the relational essence is something they give up to enter professional ministry. I'm not saying this is fair, but it's real.

It's hard enough in non-professional ministry to have authentic, deep adult friendships; in ministry, it's seemingly impossible. It would be a rare minister who had a friend in their church that they could be totally real with. If you have this, consider yourself having found the relational needle in the ministry haystack. However, regardless of the rarity of this covenantal friendship, make it a consistent part of your prayer life and ask others to join you in this prayer.

Every David needs a Jonathan. "Faithful are the wounds of a friend; profuse are the kisses of an enemy. Wounds from a sincere friend are better than many kisses from an enemy" (Prov 27:6). Let's look at the qualities of a covenantal or Jonathan-like friend.

Jonathan qualities:

- **Sacrificial**. In 1 Sam 18:4, we read that Jonathan gave David his clothes and military garb. The significance of this gift was that Jonathan recognized that David would one day be king of Israel. Rather than being envious or jealous, Jonathan submitted to God's will and sacrificed his right to the throne.
- **Loyal**. In 1 Sam 19:1–3, we read of Jonathan's loyalty toward and defense of David. King Saul told his followers to kill David. Jonathan rebuked his father and recalled David's faithfulness to him in killing Goliath.
- **Safe**. Jonathan and David were also free to express their emotions with one another. In 1 Sam 20, we read of a plan concocted by Jonathan to reveal his father's plans toward David. Jonathan was going to practice his archery. If he told his servant that the arrows he shot were to the side of the target, David was safe. If Jonathan told his servant that the arrows were beyond the target, David was to leave and not return. Jonathan told the servant that the arrows were beyond the target, meaning that David should flee. After releasing his servant, Jonathan found David, and the two men cried together.

Finding and activating one Jonathan covenantal friendship is rare. However, you may have, like I have had, the joy of collecting several Jonathans into a "covenant crew." This potential expansion of the "crew" is where you slowly add people to your covenantal friendship circle with the approval of your current covenantal friends. This crew cannot be arbitrarily established by a denomination or supervising agency. It must be organic. And if you are betrayed or have to leave your covenantal friend or crew, don't give up praying for the Spirit to provide for you. Be hypervigilant for possible covenantal friendships.

There is a good illustration that applies here. There was this cat who loved to prance around on the countertops in the kitchen and sit anywhere he wanted. One day, the cat sat on a hot stove eye. Bounding down and finding a bit of water to cool his tail in, the cat said to himself, "I'll never sit again." The moral of the story is that the problem wasn't the sitting, it was where he sat. If you get burned by someone you thought was a covenantal friend, don't give up covenantal friendships; find a better friend.

In addition to or in the absence of covenant friends, make sure you have a formal mentor or counselor on the hook. Even if you have covenant friends, having a mentor and/or counselor in your relational network is an essential survival tactic of wise ministry. The smallest of Christian community is better than no community at all.

To me, John Wesley was a master at understanding and operationalizing the theology of Christian community. Wesley demanded that those in his charge be united by transparent, accountable, supportive, and healing societies, bands, or, as some called them, Holy Clubs. These were basically what we might call small or life groups today. However, in my experience, our holy clubs typically consist of small talk, fellowship, a Bible lesson, prayer, and more small talk. This surface expression of community would have been fine for Wesley, except that he introduced an element that would make most of us want to avoid his band meetings: pointed, introspective questions. He published those questions for use in Methodist meetings in 1781 through *The Arminian* magazine.[25]

Keep in mind that Wesley believed sins are confessed to Christ for forgiveness (1 John 1:9), whereas sins are confessed to each other for healing (Jas 5:16).

Here are Wesley's five one-on-one covenantal friendship questions:

1. What known sins have you committed since our last meeting?
2. What temptations have you met with?
3. How were you delivered?
4. What have you thought, said, or done that you doubt whether it was sin or not?

25. Culbertson, "Resources."

The Uniqueness and Danger of Ministry

5. Are you keeping any secrets?

The following twenty-two questions were for larger groups of people interacting in a Christian community:

1. Am I consciously or unconsciously creating the impression that I am better than I really am? In other words, am I a hypocrite?
2. Am I honest in all my acts and words, or do I exaggerate?
3. Do I confidentially pass on to another what was told to me in confidence?
4. Can I be trusted?
5. Am I a slave to dress, friends, work, or habits?
6. Am I self-conscious, self-pitying, or self-justifying?
7. Does the Bible live in me today?
8. Do I give it time to speak to me every day?
9. Am I enjoying prayer?
10. When did I last speak to someone else about my faith?
11. Do I pray about the money I spend?
12. Do I get to bed on time and get up on time?
13. Do I disobey God in anything?
14. Do I insist upon doing something about which my conscience is uneasy?
15. Am I defeated in any part of my life?
16. Am I jealous, impure, critical, irritable, touchy, or distrustful?
17. How do I spend my spare time?
18. Am I proud?
19. Do I thank God that I am not like other people, especially the Pharisees, who despised the publican?
20. Is there anyone whom I fear, dislike, disown, criticize, hold a resentment toward, or disregard? If so, what am I doing about it?
21. Do I grumble or complain constantly?
22. Is Christ real to me?

The Work of Ministerial Soul Health

Challenge: Ask these questions often to your spouse.

The individual would ask these questions to themselves in private, and then be asked by others in public. Goodness, that is raw covenantal community!

Imagine having relationships dedicated to this kind of safe soul-keeping. Do you have even one of this kind of relationship in your life? I didn't for many years in ministry, but I am so grateful that I've got them now. They are precious to me and I cherish them. Pray hard that God give you the interest to have them, the vision to see them, and the courage to engage them with tenacious intention.

After reading the previous material, I want to give you visual folks a picture of Christian soul health.

Notice how a hummingbird's body remains still while all the rushing movement surrounds it. What a picture of the non-anxious soul, moving quickly, working hard, but with a centered, unshakable peace. A soul-healthy life is not without ambition, efficiency, or hard work. It is, however, a life without earthly attachments and centered on stillness through intentionally consistent conditioning over time.

A healthy soul can run through an airport to make a connection in peace. A healthy soul can feed a baby, prepare a meal, switch clothes, and walk the dog—all while remaining centered and still in their soul. A healthy soul can run a busy small business with a peace that passes all understanding. A healthy soul is the invisible image of God present in the chaos of post-Gen 3 life on earth.

I do not believe that becoming a centered, non-anxious person is easy. No doubt, becoming a healthy soul takes significant effort. Impediments to soul health abound in this broken world. These impediments will confront us daily from the physical realm and the realm of nefarious powers and principalities. To wrap up this chapter, let's focus on two of the most prominent impediments to soul health.

Impediment One: Living a Double-Souled Life

The most significant hindrance to being a holistically healthy human, as God originally designed, is living a divided life by segregating the physical from the spiritual. In other words, this represents the traditional secular-sacred antithesis.

One way to read the book of James regarding double-mindedness is to recognize the divided loyalties as those between the secular and sacred, the kingdom of the world and the kingdom of God. James 1:8 reads that such a person (with divided loyalty) is double-minded and unstable in all they do. In Jas 4:8, we read, "Come close to God, and God will come close to you. Wash your hands, you sinners; purify your hearts, for your loyalty is divided between God and the world."

The Greek word for "double-minded" in both these verses is *dipsychos* (dip'-soo-khos), from the root words "*dis*" for double and "*psychē*" (psoo-khay') for soul.[26] The meaning is interpreted as double-souled, split-souled, fractured-soul, or dissociated-soul.[27]

Remember the holistic vision of an original soul earlier in the chapter. A soul that is illustrated by concentric circles emanating from the epicenter of a will surrendered to God's will, contextualized in God's kingdom. And then contrast that integrated soul with a double-minded, fractured-soul, disintegrated soul, where all the circles exist in conflict with each other and God. Loyalties are disordered, divided, and lacking synergy and alignment in the disintegrated soul. The most debilitating effect of sinfulness and impediment to soul health is the disintegration of the human soul. A disintegrated, divided soul lives as if there are two distinct realms: the physical and the spiritual, sacred, and secular. This disintegration is the pathogen of original sin, dividing creation and Creator, heaven and earth, causing our soul disease. Disintegration is death!

---

26. *Thayer's Greek Lexicon*.

27. My interpretation is extrapolated from The NIV Application Commentary on James: Nystrom, *James*, loc. 229.

The Work of Ministerial Soul Health

Let's think of this another way to drive the point home. Consider your life a collection of zones, such as food, play, work, household chores, church, pets, Bible reading, sports, and prayer. We move in and out of these life zones throughout the day.

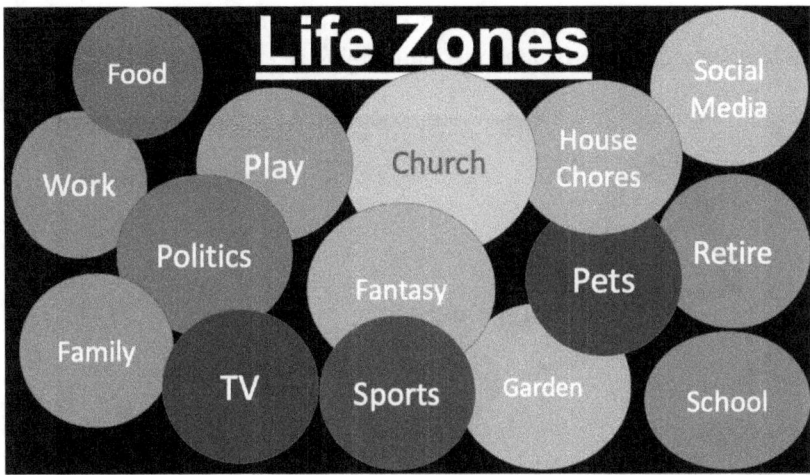

Yet we unconsciously divide these life zones into two categories: the sacred and the secular. And because of our bifurcated Greek sacred/secular anthropology, which is decidedly not Hebraic holistic anthropology, we embrace this divided living as normal. It can be visualized as in the following graphic.

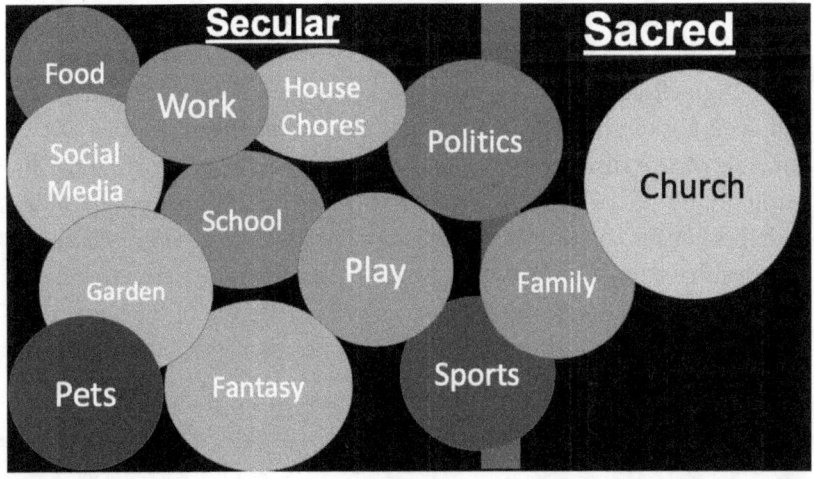

In our Western Greek vision of life, work, lawn maintenance, sex, household chores, and other aspects of daily life are placed on the secular side of life. However, church, Bible reading, prayer, and family are clearly on the sacred side, along with perhaps sports and politics. You undoubtedly know people, maybe yourself, who place sports and political affiliation in the sacred side of life. Regardless of what you put on what side of life, sacred or secular, a divided, disintegrated human life is death.

The theological foundation here builds upon the biblical Hebraic anthropology of Gen 2, affirming that God's original purpose is for the whole person, both physically and spiritually, to live without divided loyalty between the physical and spiritual realms, between heaven and earth, and between the sacred and secular.

Originally, the physical and spiritual realms were perfectly integrated and synergistic. The two were not mutually antagonistic, despite the arguments of Docetists, Gnostics, and Manichaeans.[28] On the contrary, the spiritual and physical realms existed in complete and perfect harmony, with this holistic creation reaching its zenith in human design.[29] Therefore, the ideal harmony between the physical and spiritual experiences in the original composition can be considered a manifestation of the perfect will of God on earth as it is in heaven. Hence, after the fall, God's teleological purpose is to redeem all aspects of life.

---

28. Oden, *Classic Christianity*, 140.
29. Wolff, *Anthropology*, 5–10.

As Erickson posits, no segment of original physical creation was devoid of spiritual significance because God is responsible for all physical and spiritual creation.[30] Because of the spiritual and physical harmony in every aspect of God's original design, it is logical to infer that the first humans were also created with the same harmonious character. Bulgakov describes the pre-fall people of God as a "divine-humanity."[31] Chan agrees that original humanity was essentially the confluence of heaven and earth's best.[32] Therefore, the entire creation embodied this synergistic integration and depended entirely upon the human-divine connection. Consequently, the biblical account of humanity's loss of connection to God after the fall in Gen 3 precipitated the instantaneous disintegration of the original creation as a holistic environment.

Because humanity is only fully alive as long as the breath or Spirit of God indwells them, losing this integrated state would ripple throughout all creation. After the fall, however, humans were disintegrated from God as their life source, and they died as God promised they would. They died because they violated the covenantal relationship of perfect integration implicit in their creation, and by association, the rest of creation died. Sin destroyed humanity's physical and spiritual integration, thus vitiating God's original creation schema. This condition doesn't have to be this way; it can be different.

> This transformation, from disintegration to integration, means that anyone who belongs to Christ has become a new person. The old [disintegrated] life is gone; a new [integrated] life has begun! This integration is a gift from God, who brought us back to himself through Christ. And God has given us the task of reconciling people to him. For God was in Christ, reconciling the world [everything] to himself, no longer counting people's sins against them. And he gave us this wonderful message of reconciliation. (2 Cor 5:17–19)

---

30. Erickson, *Christian Theology*, 371.
31. Bulgakov, *Bride of the Lamb*, loc. 3935.
32. Chan, *Liturgical Theology*, 23.

The Uniqueness and Danger of Ministry

The following image is a vision of the abundant life Jesus spoke of.

I believe that the solution to the sacred-secular problem has never been more beautifully put than the way A. W. Tozer put it: "Let a person sanctify the Lord God in their heart, and they can thereafter perform no common act. To that person, every act will be sacred and the whole world a sanctuary."[33]

Soul health is an integrated life. Soul health is a holistic, Christlike life. Minister, we can't lead somewhere we've never been or don't live. The challenge of living an integrated life is our matter before we make it a matter for God's people. Everything that has come before in this book is an invitation to live in holistic integration and lead God's people in that direction. There is no hurrying this process. Shocker, hurry is the next major impediment to soul health.

Impediment Two: A Hurried Soul

Defining a hurried lifestyle will be helpful before I move on. A hurried life, or hurry sickness as I've heard it called, is a habit of thinking and feeling characterized by continual rushing and anxiousness. Sword and Zimbardo characterize hurry sickness as "a dis-ease in which a person feels chronically short of time, and so tends to perform every task faster, getting flustered

---

33. Tozer, *Pursuit of God*, 92.

when encountering any kind of delay."[34] Do I hear an "Amen!" Yeah, I thought so; no amen from me, either. I have lived so hurriedly sick for most of my life. The famous psychiatrist Carl Jung said, "Hurry is not *of* the devil; hurry *is* the devil."[35] I am convinced that time is the first challenge you will face as a person and pastor in achieving contentment. People are too busy and hurried to live emotionally healthy, spiritually rich, and vibrant lives.

You know you live a hurried life:

- When you jump checkout lines because the one you're in moves too slowly
- When you multitask in the bathroom
- When you set reminders for your reminders
- When you lose sleep over your schedule
- When people just won't get to the point
- When eating, putting on makeup, and driving coexist

The Charleston Southern University School of Business conducted the *Obstacles to Growth Survey*, which included over twenty thousand Christians from around the globe and identified busyness as a significant distraction from spiritual life. Listen carefully to their hypothesis:

> It may be the case that Christians are assimilating (syncretizing) to a culture of busyness, hurry, and overload, which leads to God becoming more marginalized in Christians' lives, which leads to a deteriorating relationship with God, which leads to Christians becoming even more vulnerable to adopting secular assumptions about how to live, which leads to more conformity to a culture of busyness, hurry and overload. And then the cycle of soul dis-ease revolves and deepens.[36]

I love the objectivity of empirical research, but the subjective living with hurry sickness gets me. I hate how those I love most often bear the brunt of my hurry sickness symptoms. John Mark Comer seems to agree with me when he writes with apparent sadness in his book *The Ruthless Elimination of Hurry*:

---

34. Sword, "Hurry Sickness."
35. Comer, *Ruthless Elimination of Hurry*, 20.
36. Zigarelli, "Distracted from God," 11.

> Hurry and love are incompatible. All my worst moments as a father, a husband, and a pastor, even as a human being, are when I'm in a hurry—late for an appointment, behind on my unrealistic to-do list, trying to cram too much into my day. I ooze anger, tension, a critical nagging—the antithesis of love.[37]

The soul health impediments of living a divided life by straddling the sacred and secular realms as well as hurry sickness are the top two impediments I've identified in my life and study. You could pile on, but that's for another medium. Comer's comment gets at the real pain of living a soul-sick life and the impact on my immediate family. Minister, you can't lead somewhere you haven't been and don't live. Changing churches won't change your soul. Only a long obedience in the same direction of intentional soul health training, rather than trying, will change your soul. I'm not talking about saving your soul for Jesus one day; I'm talking about changing your soul into the soul of Jesus right now. And the first place I want the soul of Jesus to show up is in my immediate family. Now, we focus on the wisdom of ministerial family soul health.

---

37. Comer, *Ruthless Elimination of Hurry*, 23.

4

The *Wisdom* of Ministerial Family Soul Health

Pastor your family better than you pastor your church!

IN THIS CHAPTER, MY wife, LaDon, and I will direct insights to the minister and the minister's wife, respectively. Some content will overlap with previous material, but this overlap will serve as reinforcement rather than redundancy. Also, you will identify with the following content to a greater or lesser degree. Some will read the following pages in confusion because the experiences we share are not your experiences. I expect that the majority will deeply resonate with the chapter's content. No matter where you land on the spectrum of content identification, take it all in stride, and let the Spirit speak to you in your life experience.

Finally, some of the stories we share may trigger intense feelings. This reaction is normal if you've suffered similar experiences. Take this response as a cue to take action for your health. Reach out to a resource in appendix 1. Share your feelings about what triggered you with a trusted friend. Secure a counselor to walk you through the hurt to the healing. Above all, do something with your response. Don't ignore it. The uniqueness and danger of ministry are like termites; prevention is best, but if you discover damage, don't ignore it, or your whole life house may crumble. Minister and minister's spouse, we love you. You're not crazy or alone.

Steve Speaking to the Minister

As significant and vocationally anchoring as a divine calling to ministry is to the minister, it is an equally important consideration for the minister's spouse. Lemme splain; yep, again, always splaining. As someone with a divine clarion call to professional ministry, my ministry vocation is anchored, like Paul on the Damascus Road, in that experience. Like you, I recall hearing the Spirit calling me to ministry as a profession. I wanted to do something else, but I can't because of that special call beyond common Christian service responsibility to professional ministry.

I became a Christian on November 17, 1980, at 9:34 p.m. in an old, beat-up brown Dodge Dart parked outside my house after a Fellowship of Christian Athletes meeting. Two years later, I won a lacrosse scholarship at Penn State, where I planned to study pre-medicine and pursue a career in sports medicine as my chosen vocation. However, my vocation of calling, not my vocation of choice, occurred while I was sitting in Algebra II class during the spring of my senior high school year. Infected with senioritis, I was daydreaming about my new college life, playing lacrosse and studying medicine, when suddenly the room lit up like a flash bomb had gone off—a soul-whiteout. All my soul's attentiveness was at its highest level ever, and I heard the voice of the Spirit clearly say to me, "You will never be happy doing anything else but telling people what I've done for you."

There was no doubt at that moment that the Spirit of God had just rerouted my entire life. I was not going off to college to study medicine but to study ministry. With continued tunnel vision, I marched to the career counselor's office and announced that I would not be studying medicine, but ministry, in college. She leaned back in her chair, removed her glasses, and said, "Well, I've never had anyone tell me that. You should find the most religious person you know and ask where it is that someone studies ministry." I took the advice, and here I am, forty-one years later, still anchoring myself week in and week out in that divine Algebra II high school moment. Every time I wanted to quit ministry and do anything else, the words of the Spirit from that divine calling moment came rushing to the front of my soul, and I dug in for another week.

The Wisdom of Ministerial Family Soul Health

As a minister, I know you've got a story of a calling like mine. But what if your spouse doesn't? Where do they find their anchor when they want to quit? Right, their marriage to you. In other words, they are called to you in a covenant marriage and by default married into ministry. Your wife may feel called to you as their spouse, but they don't feel called generally to professional ministry or specifically to your current ministry context. In this case, if you quit professional ministry and took up another trade, your spouse wouldn't feel compelled to advance in ministerial credentialing or education. My wife and I have spoken to many ministry spouses about this, and most are emphatic that if aliens abducted their minister spouse, they would not seek a future in professional ministry. Furthermore, many state that they would avoid marrying another minister.

To be clear, every Christian is a minister, but is every Christian a *minister*? I don't think so. Whereas every Christian is responsible to serve in ministry, few are called out of fundamental Christian responsibility into professional ministry. Many followed Christ as disciples, but only a few were called out of the crowd of disciples to be *disciples*. Although you may want to debate this point theologically, you'll need to go along with me here if you're going to understand our orientation toward soul health for the minister's family. You may want to track back to chapter one, where I review the idea of calling more broadly.

Moving on from the concept of calling, I've come to understand that marriage is generally assisted living for men. When my wife leaves for any significant length of time (more than three hours), she should schedule an assisted living service to help me with the day-to-day tasks. I love her. Pairing the general need of Christian men to have a life helpmate through marriage, as in Gen 2:18 (translation: helpmate as life coach), is a covenantal blessing. However, with the realities of professional ministry, an official assisted living helpmate in marriage often expands into an unofficial assistant in ministry. This absorption into professional ministry occurs regardless of the minister's spouse having a call to professional ministry or not.

Making the non-calling of many ministers' wives more of a complex challenge is that, most often, professional ministry positions have an unspoken "two for one" expectation attached. Consider that your wife may be at the church you pastor because she's not allowed to worship anywhere else due to your position. Ask your wife, "If I were a volunteer, serving in church as a non-ministry professional, would you want to attend the church we currently attend?" Don't get sensitive about her response. If her answer was

The Uniqueness and Danger of Ministry

"no," it's not an indictment of your leadership or preaching prowess; it's far more likely because she would like to go to church for once as a person, not the pastor's wife.

Part of the problem here is that the professional minister, like the professional accountant or electrician, moves through their training without their significant other. Furthermore, the minister's significant other may be undergoing professional training in business or nursing, with little to no training in what will become their primary vocation through marriage, that of professional ministry. Most ministers' wives don't have much training or mentorship before or during their spouse's ministry career. Church organization leaders should consider providing equal yet distinctive training and mentorship for ministers' wives, as they support their husbands. I'm not talking about requiring master of divinity degrees for wives of ministers, but at least build into the organization's culture, equal training and support, nurturing systemic attention to and space for ministers' spouses.

It's crucial to recognize that the majority of minister spouses are not on the verge of hospitalization or moral failure due to their marriage to a minister. The majority of those married to a minister know intuitively that ministry is the highest vocational priority in their lives. Ministers' wives are willingly, faithfully serving the local church and the kingdom of God at large. I'm not attempting to characterize all pastors' wives as conscripted, enslaved people trudging through the work of professional ministry week in and week out. However, I am trying to reveal the realities of ministry for the minister's wife that are so often left unsung. If your spouse identifies with any of this chapter, she is not crazy or alone in her understanding. The struggle is real, and the uniqueness and danger of ministry need to be normalized and addressed.

Let me emphasize again that professional ministry is not unique and dangerous for the ministry family because someone is doing something wrong. Ministry is intrinsically unique and dangerous. Despite the intrinsic nature of professional ministry, most ministry spouses I speak with affirm a palpable sense of ministry nobility, as I described previously when writing about ministers as professionals. Take, for example, the wife of Pastor Eugene Peterson. Pastor Peterson describes his wife's sense of mutual commitment (notice I didn't say "call") to ministry:

> For Jan, "pastor's wife" was not just being married to a pastor; it was far more vocational than that, a way of life. It meant participation in an intricate web of hospitality, living at the intersection of

human need and God's grace, inhabiting a community where men and women who didn't fit were welcomed, where neglected children were noticed, and where the stories of Jesus were told. People who thought they had no stories found that they had stories that were part of the Jesus story. Being a pastor's wife would place her strategically yet unobtrusively at a heavily trafficked intersection between heaven and earth.[1]

However, to press the calling point, what if the ministry spouse has no divine calling story to anchor themselves in when the winds of ministry threaten to capsize the ministry-family ship? Wow, how the ministry wind threatens us at times.

I recall again the minister who shared a story with me about a Saturday eighteen months earlier, when he was at the church for another critical ministry event. His wife texted him that she was taking the kids to the store. She never came back. Eventually, she told him she couldn't take life as a married woman to a professional minister anymore. As they talked, she revealed that being married to a professional minister was like being in a polygamous relationship where she was always the second wife behind the first wife of the church. To her, the church was her public husband's mistress. She declared she would never play second fiddle again in marriage. She wanted to be married to him, and wanted him to be married to her, but never realized the powerful allure of the church as his mistress. This woman served in the church generally as a responsible Christian (volunteer), yet didn't have a call as a professional minister. In other words, she served the ministry, but was not in ministry. Pastor, is your spouse playing first or second fiddle? Don't rely on your hunch to know how they would answer; ask them.

Perhaps only a politician's spouse comes close to the uniqueness and danger of a minister's spouse role. Spouses of politicians indeed are swept up in the vocation of their politician spouse. Some politicians' spouses have a sense of calling to politics, but not all do. Not all spouses of politicians relish the scrutiny and pressure that come with being in the public eye. The parallels between politics and ministry are dramatic. Still, they lack one element that takes the uniqueness and danger of marriage to a professional minister well beyond that of a politician: the eternal stakes.

When the apostle Paul described his many trials as a professional minister, the one "last straw" type burden he punctuated his speech with was the eternal nature of the church. He could endure and did endure many

---

1. Peterson, *Pastor*, 314.

trials, but the heaviest one was the concern for the church on his shoulders. Paul was not married, but if he were, his spouse would feel the same eternal weight of ministry. Imagine bearing this burden without a call to ministry as a soul anchor for ministry work when the going got tough.

No other vocation is as immersive as professional ministry for marriage. In what other vocation does the spouse feel such spiritual and eternal pressure to be a good minister's spouse? Does an accountant's spouse feel heavy spiritual and eternal pressure in the frozen food aisle of the grocery store to interact effectively and effusively with one of her spouse's accounting clients? Would they even know who their accountant spouse's clients were? The minister's spouse and everything in their soul would immediately stand to attention if they turned down the frozen food aisle and saw a church member in the same ice cream section they were about to enter. Do plumbers' spouses feel pressured to put on a "joy of the Lord" game face when going to the Little League field, knowing they will encounter plumbing clients? Do truck drivers, daycare workers, loan officers, or hotel managers' spouses feel the eternal weight of their spouse's profession? Not likely. Listen to some of the actual research on the subject.

Research suggests that the traditional expectations for clergy spouses are both increasingly less realistic and a source of stress within clergy marriages.[2] A woman married to a parish pastor must not only deal with the role-conflict and overload associated with being a contemporary woman, but she must also contend with the unrealistic expectations associated with her role as the minister's spouse.[3] Furthermore,

> In observing pastors' wives in clinical interviews, workshops, retreats, and support groups, researchers have found frequent complaints concerning the many additional roles and high standards of role performance expected of them. These demands are often further compounded by the high visibility and accessibility of the pastorate. The high-performance expectations placed upon them by congregations and church officials, as well as their self-imposed high expectations and lack of clarity regarding specific role expectations, result in reduced quality of life for many women married to clergy. This burden is frequently evidenced by self-reported confusion, tension, and emotional stress, and by the high incidence of burnout and loneliness observed by others.[4]

2. Nesbitt, "Marriage, Parenthood."
3. Baker, "Predictors of Well-Being."
4. Baker, "Predictors of Well-Being," 33.

Whether by divine calling or marriage into professional ministry, the uniqueness and dangers are palpable among ministry spouses, albeit often unspoken. What follows are a few nuggets of wisdom from a minister's perspective to safeguard your family in ministry.

Nugget One: Pastor your family better than you pastor your church, by prioritizing them appropriately.

I know this will take great courage, but come on, brace up and ask your wife the following question. Tell her not to think, just respond with the first answer that comes to mind.

- Does your husband pastor you and your family better than they pastor their church?

    Not very well 1....3....5 Somewhat well....7....10 Absolutely great

OK, this could be awkward. You might want to take some time to unpack this with your spouse before moving on.

Listen to Paul David Tripp share in his must-read book *Dangerous Calling*, what he calls an all too common reality in the homes of ministry families. He sets up the story of a church hiring a new pastor, and after several months, the church realizes that something is amiss. After several more weeks, the pastor calls an emergency leadership meeting to share what is going on with his family. This revelation was the ultimatum the pastor's wife gave the pastor: "It's me or your ministry. You have to choose one or the other, because you're not going to have both." She went on to say that she could not do it anymore. She couldn't deal with the vast disconnect between their public and private lives. She said she was exhausted with pretending that things were okay when they were anything but okay. She was tired of hearing her husband consistently call people to do things he wasn't doing. She hated the new city she lived in and bitterly reminded her husband that she had begged him not to uproot her and the children. Having unloaded on him, she then told him that she would not be in church on Sunday or any other Sunday to come. It was "done, over," and he would have to make her and the children the focus of his attention "for the first time in many years."[5] Uh, oh!

---

5. Tripp. *Dangerous Calling*, 60.

Ensure your spouse knows they are in the first chair for the fiddle section of your marriage. Overtly and emphatically state this in all church leadership venues possible, including the pulpit. Make it uncomfortably known that your spouse plays the first fiddle in your life. Again, "fiddle," what's up with that?

During my long-term pastorate in Maryland, I learned a few things about prioritizing my wife and family in the context of the church the hard way. First, we designed our covenant partnership (membership) course to include a segment where my wife and I would set boundaries for the church and our family. This venue is where I establish Sabbath boundaries; additionally, I set time and geographic boundaries. I explained that our house was not their house. Don't drop by our house unannounced. Don't imagine that I'm available 24/7 to the church. I am available 24/7 to my bio-family, but not to my church family. Here, I explained that our church has developed and trained effective leadership beyond me, the pastor, so that the church leadership can be available to the church family 24/7, not just me alone. I, of course, communicated this to the classes with kindness and often comedy. I want to empower you to set these boundaries kindly but emphatically.

During this new members' type class, my wife would take time to talk about our children. She kindly but clearly stated that she did not believe that she needed a village to raise her child. She emphasized that there have been too many village idiots who have attempted to raise our children in the past, and we'll own our child-rearing ourselves. Sometimes, the room would become uncomfortable when she let those potential covenant partners know that they didn't have to police our children's behavior.

Nugget Two: Intentionally and emphatically set expectations early regarding your wife and family's role in church.

Setting expectations early with church leadership for your spouse's ministry engagement and the quality of that engagement is a savvy approach to ministry leadership. For instance, if your spouse has a divine call to ministry, it would be wise for the minister to allow their spouse to explain their ministry calling early in the ministry appointment, so all leadership would be clear about the minister's spouse's professional ministry role, even if unpaid. On the other hand, if the minister's spouse does not have a call to professional ministry, except through marriage, it will be equally important to inform the leadership of this.

In the case of a spouse without a divine call to professional ministry, the congregation will need to understand that, although the pastor's wife may not have had a Damascus Road calling to professional ministry like her husband, her role will still be one of unique influence due to the holy assignment she has accepted through her helpmate role to the pastor.[6] This holy assignment, and its unique influence, needs to be clearly defined between the minister and spouse. Consider consulting with a more seasoned ministry couple with a similar marriage relationship to ministry for clarification on ministry roles and influence. If you are a denominational leader, I am begging you to please enhance the developmental programs for current and future pastors' wives.

When I say influence, I mean that my wife, although not having a call to professional ministry in her life, was equally invested in the health and well-being of the church I pastored. She carried the same burden for the souls we pastored. We were in ministry together. Therefore, I wanted her to have the freedom to represent my pastoral authority if she believed it was in the best interest of the church. I trust my wife to have my back and represent my leadership authority. The ministry couple is in it together, that is, in ministry together to varying degrees, unlike marriage, which is a complete mutual commitment. Varying degrees of influence and responsibility will depend on negotiating with your wife as to how much and what kind of influence she is interested in having. Be flexible and revisit this issue often to maintain a united front. Remember, through divine calling or marriage, you're in it together.

Another nuance of this second point is ensuring that church leadership does not expect the minister's spouse and children to serve as the benchmark for spirituality within the church. One such instance is when our elementary school-aged daughter was on the church's balcony during a Sunday worship service with one of her friends. The girls were getting a little too exuberant during one of the songs. A church person scolded my daughter for what they called "booty dancing." They continued with the scolding by emphasizing that the church would be very disappointed in the pastor's daughter if she carried on like she was. My daughter came to my

---

6. LaDon picked up this notion of a "holy assignment" from Pastor Syrah Vergana of the Lahaina, Hawaii, Church of God when we were conducting a soul health clinic with regional ministers.

The Uniqueness and Danger of Ministry

wife and confessed her "booty dancing," worried that it might negatively impact my position as pastor. Thankfully, my wife handled the situation expertly, putting the woman in her place and reassuring our daughter that the woman's behavior was unacceptable. Setting expectations in advance with church leadership and the congregation empowers you and your wife to enforce boundaries with leadership and church folks systemically and spontaneously.

As mentioned above, what other spouses and children have to face such unique and dangerous aspects of their spouses' or parents' vocation, and where they worship no less?

Nugget Three: Establish a pattern for handling church conflict.

You and your family will often experience church conflict together. Your wife and kids will undoubtedly be confronted with conflicts happening in the church at all levels. You're not doing anything wrong; it's the intrinsic immersive nature of being a ministry family. However, this conflict cannot become a toxic "us versus them" relationship where your negative emotions become their negative emotions. Negotiate with your wife about what conflicts they want to be privy to and what conflicts they don't. If this is clear in your marriage, then in selected cases you will inform her, and in other cases you will not. Your wife must agree to the conflict awareness terms. As for the children, church conflict needs to be processed in a manner appropriate to the children's age and maturity. Don't lay out the gritty details of the youth pastor's infidelity and how you went about firing them at dinner with your middle school child present; of course, duh! But don't avoid processing the youth pastor's firing either. Primarily, ensure that addressing church conflict is a united front, with you and your spouse working together as much as possible. Now, if you're the youth pastor who was fired, this will be even trickier. Good luck with that one.

Church conflict processed in a healthy way with the ministry family will inoculate your family against the negative associations that ministry families often form in the context of church work. I can't count the number of pastors' kids we have spoken with who recount stories of how their parents were hurt, and these now-grown adults are still struggling with those incidents of church hurt and their current capacity to have affection for the church. Overall, it is best not to air church difficulties with children. The goal is to raise children to be the next church leaders, who will love God and the church, and then go on to raise their families to do the same. When the children are age-appropriate, church struggles can be used as a learning tool for how to be Christlike, even under challenging situations.

Valuing your spouse as a priority over the church, setting clear boundaries and expectations with leadership, and processing church conflict together as a united front will all help your ministry family float rather than fight, rafting along the ministry river despite the rough rapids you will often encounter together.

Nugget Four: Empower your spouse to hold you accountable.

Ensure that your spouse knows they have the right to enforce boundaries in professional ministry-life balance. Ministers are notorious for being oblivious to the marginlessness of ministry. Early in ministry, my wife often asked what evenings and Saturdays I had available for marriage dates, friends' time out, or family excursions. During that phase of ministry life, I often answered, "Well, I'm not sure, honey. Let me get through the staff meeting this week and my planning time, and I'll see if I can carve out some time." It wasn't long before my wife had to have a "come to Jesus" meeting with me, setting firm boundaries in place for our home and family. Those kinds of meetings thankfully registered as wake-up calls for me.

However, it still took me several years of wake-up calls to reprogram myself and my leadership in the art of prioritizing ministry margin-making for my family. Remember, ministry is immersive, not because you're doing something wrong, but because it just is. It will suffocate you and your family slowly, almost imperceptibly, until it's too late. Don't succumb to the carbon monoxide of ministry: marginlessness. Encourage your spouse to speak authoritatively into your life regarding the importance of margin in ministry.

Nugget Five: You can't subcontract your family's soul health; own it.

Get this, you are entirely responsible to your marital and family soul health. I say responsible "to" rather than "for" because you can't make anyone healthy in soul. You can only provide the context and opportunity for your wife and kids to be nurtured by your leadership. Remember, pastor your family better than you pastor your church. This principle may seem obvious, but, as I've said repeatedly, no one gets lucky with soul health. Just because you and your family work the family business of ministry does not mean that you and your family are close to God. Pastor, be creative with your co-pastor wife in creating a nurturing context of soul health for your family.

In a state of palpable regret, an older minister recently told me that he was stunned his children weren't serving God as adults. He emphasized how dumbfounded he was that this could happen, given that he took his kids to church every weekend, midweek, and during special events. All their friends were primarily church kids. What could have possibly gone wrong with so much church immersion? During a conversation with one of his kids, they opened up about ministry life and informed their ministry dad that they had never experienced going to church with their dad; they always went to work with him. Ouch!

Church isn't always a magical ministry kingdom where ministry families, by sheer osmosis, fall in love with Jesus and live happily ever after. Ministry may be that for some, but not most, according to my experience and research. As with any other Christian family, parents must take responsibility for their family's spiritual well-being, as well as their physical health. I'm confident that the reader can assess their family's physical health and feel good about their concerted efforts to care for it by mindfully paying attention to reasonably healthy meals, regular medical check-ups, home security, and safe driving habits. Only the most out-of-touch parents would blame their child's lack of physical health on a doctor for not coming to the house more consistently to check in on their child's physical health. Reasonable parents would sense responsibility to their children's general physical health. Of course, on rare occasions, kids are born with congenital disabilities or succumb to unavoidable accidents. However, for normal physical health, parents are responsible to their family's physical well-being.

The same should be true for the spiritual well-being of the family. Only the out-of-touch minister would blame the church for the lack in their kids' spiritual health because they didn't show up more consistently at home to model the life of Jesus before their kids or have family devotions. The minister and the minister's spouse exclusively own the soul health of themselves and their young children. You are the chief evangelist and disciple maker of your child. However, eventually, each child has to decide what they'll do with Christ. Even with the best soul-health parenting, some children will just reject Jesus. There is a hell, and some choose to go there despite their parents' efforts. The point is that merely taking your kids to church/work with you multiple times a week does not necessarily mean that soul health is taking root. Christian ministry parents, keep your eyes open and often create a distinction between working for God and living with God in your home.

Nugget Six: Believe that God's got your back, so you can have the courage to do what's best for your family even if the church doesn't like it.

Here is an example from my life as a lead pastor. There was a time in my ministry leadership when several years passed without robust and positive youth ministry leadership. This situation was due to unfortunate hires on my part. Ministers notoriously hire too quickly and fire too slowly.

When this negative trend started, one of my kids was just entering the youth ministry. Our child was not connecting to the youth ministry. My wife noticed our child struggling spiritually and frequently seemed disconnected. She brought this to my attention. I expressed that I was doing my best to negotiate better leadership but needed time. She was patient to a point, which is her spiritual gift. However, her concern for our child crossed the threshold of her patience. Even though my wife was a prominent figure in church ministry, highly engaged in music ministry and life group leadership, she informed me she would be stepping down from some responsibilities. She said she would be continuing to attend our first Sunday service; however, during the second service, she would be taking our child to another church youth group where he could connect spiritually. She and our child did exactly this until I was able to hire a youth pastor who could provide a positive spiritual experience for him. She was not willing to sacrifice our child. I'm sure you can imagine the position I was in.

This youth ministry situation was certainly not what I had planned, but it was still my responsibility, and I couldn't fix it quickly. I was confronted with a "rock and hard place" leadership challenge. My wife was never ugly or cavalier about the position I was in, but she was firmly for our child over my ministry. She is beautifully wise that way. Therefore, I joined her in this stance and informed our church leadership, presenting our united marital front, about what was happening, so that if questions arose, as they did, about my wife and child's attendance, they could answer confidently. This situation lasted over a year. We lost a couple of families, not because my wife and child attended another church during this leadership crisis, but because of the same reasons we shared about the effect this leadership crisis could have on our child. We survived, and my child thrived. Not every story I have in ministry family life resulted in a definitively positive outcome.

The key here is that you realize and firmly embrace the fact that no one else owns your soul health or that of your family. Have the courage to do what's best for your family, even if your church doesn't like it.

Nugget Seven: Make soul health planning a nonnegotiable family experience.

Soul health planning for the minister and the ministry family should be a nonnegotiable spiritual discipline for you and your family. As mentioned earlier, ministerial soul health planning is not a ministry/church soul health plan, but rather a ministerial soul health plan specifically for the minister. Soul health planning should be implemented first in the life of the minister and marriage, then generalized to the family. The next soul health plan that should be designed beyond the minister's SHP is the SHP of the minister's family.

The process is primarily the same for the ministry family as for the minister. However, a significant difference is front-loaded in soul health planning for the ministry family. Independent of each other, both spouses should spend time with the Holy Spirit to discern an overarching soul goal and soul word for the family SHP. Eventually, as a couple, compare soul goals and words—synthesizing them is wise. Loads of resources are provided in appendix 2 and at www.ministryoasis.com.

Develop soul exercises and personal practices that align with your family's soul goal and word in this collaborative context. These exercises and practices may or may not relate to the individual SHPs of the husband and wife. However, one exercise must be included in the family SHP, that of the Sabbath. Moreover, the couple must be united in their priority for the Sabbath. You may have to make tough decisions about Saturday sports, church engagements, theater show runs, or friends' birthday parties. My recommendation is not to be overly rigid in your Sabbath planning; instead, give the Sabbath a prominent place in your family's life, but not a legalistic one. For instance, if you are traveling, you may not observe the Sabbath that week. Another aspect of flexible Sabbath keeping is that you may need to move your Sabbath to another day from time to time. If you curate family

Sabbath effectively and can start young, your children will likely grow to cherish Sabbath as a sweet bonding time with God and each other.

A word of caution about introducing the Sabbath in a family context where children are already in middle school: proceed carefully and adopt a posture of flexibility. It's very possible that your middle/high schooler may not have the biblical urgency about Sabbath that you do. If you plan to incorporate Sabbath into your family routine, navigate this time fluidly and find the best course for your family's Sabbath experience. Remember, the principle of the Sabbath for Jesus is that the Sabbath was made for you, not you for the Sabbath. Relax about family soul health planning, but don't get sloppy.

Okay, that was seven nuggets of soul health advice from one minister to another. Now for the main dish.

By the way, as I hand the content over to LaDon, you may wonder why I often refer to the minister's wife and not spouse. That's because in my experience and research, the male spouse of a minister is generally not held to the same expectations and standards as a female spouse of a minister.[7] Consequently, it seems reasonable to hear from a female minister's spouse as a subject matter expert. With that said, here's LaDon.

LaDon Speaking to Ministers and Ministers' Spouses

The loneliest person on the planet is the pastor's wife.

—Dr. Sam Chand

The Church of God denomination (Cleveland, Tennessee) hosts the Top 200 conference every year. The Top 200 invitation is based on an ABC metric of Attendance, Buildings, and Cash. In 2019, Steve and I were once again invited to attend in Atlanta, Georgia, hosted at the historic Mt. Paran Church of God. The keynote speaker for the conference was Dr. Sam Chand, a renowned author who serves pastors, ministries, and businesses as a leadership architect and change strategist. According to ministry leaders Steve and I know, Chand is the real deal with street credibility and degrees to back up the value of his opinion.

As that conference was ending, Chand was asked what would be an indispensable nugget of secret pastoral insight he couldn't leave without imparting to the ministers in the audience. His words were starkly

---

7. Daniel, "Pastor's Husband."

The Uniqueness and Danger of Ministry

straightforward. I was stunned to hear him say, "The loneliest person on the planet is the pastor's wife."[8] After all the leadership advice and ministry strategy direction, this was the indispensable takeaway!!!

He said this previously unsung reality out loud. I knew it to be true because I had lived it. I have spoken with many friends who have expressed loneliness as a decisive factor in their dissatisfaction with professional ministry. Chand's point was the very first time I had ever heard an influential ministry leader share concern for the pastor's wife. This public recognition of my private experience marked the beginning of my realization that I am not alone in the loneliness of professional ministry as the spouse of a minister. There is ample research confirming the reality of ministerial spouse loneliness.[9] One such article states it emphatically like this: "Loneliness was the single most common complaint, often voiced by spouses who were otherwise happy. Others were severely lonely and are looking forward to their spouse's retirement or are considering a divorce."[10]

While loneliness may be a significant struggle for the pastor's wife, I do not believe she has to be alone in her loneliness. I believe a pastor's wife can put practices in place to mitigate the negative impact of the intrinsic loneliness and any other dissatisfying aspects of ministry. The following pages may at times feel like a miserable slog through the muck of ministry, and it is. I would love just to share only the mountaintop experiences, and there are many. But to do so would short-circuit the first step in any kind of healing and recognition that there is something to be healed. So hang in there with me. I'm not just venting, I'm verbalizing the reality to varying degrees many pastors' wives live with week in and week out, in hopes that you know you're not crazy or alone. Healing is the destination, but I've got to start with the hurt.

In the ministerial soul health clinics we conduct out of Ministry Oasis,[11] we hear the following at every event, that the pastor's wife remains silent about her struggles connected to the ministry. It is like a silent scream, a muffled bellowing in many pastors' homes. These comments, and my own experience, reminded me of that line out of the movie *The Village*: "These are the things we do not speak of."[12] You just don't talk about it. Who

---

8. Sam Chand at the Church of God Top 200 conference, Atlanta, Georgia, 2018.
9. Baker, "Predictors of Well-Being."
10. Murphy-Geiss, *Clergy Spouses and Families*, 15.
11. www.ministryoasis.com.
12. Shyamalan, *The Village*.

would understand the role/job description anyway? I remember trying to explain my role to women who attended our church. They could never wrap their minds around the heavy weight of eternity that is felt for every person under the pastor's wife's influence. Not to mention the unrealistic list of expectations associated with the role. Like it or not, many women in the congregation need something specific from the pastor's wife. Often, the needs range from needing a mother figure, confidant, best friend, counselor, sounding board, and on and on. Realistically, no one can be all these things to everyone.

 I have served in ministry my entire life and want to give some perspective on my connection to ministry. First, as a PK (preacher's kid), I grew up attending and serving in the church where my father served as pastor. As a middle schooler, I worked in a bus ministry every Saturday, inviting children to church, and on Sunday, I rode the bus to pick them up. I worked in the children's church, sang in the choir, sang solos, cleaned the church, and did my best not to do anything to tarnish my father's ministry. In the summer of my tenth-grade year of high school, my father accepted the call of God to become a missionary to Haiti, where my title changed to MK (missionary kid). Secondly, after college, I married a minister who attended and served in churches, accepting positions as youth pastor, discipleship director, associate pastor, and ultimately, lead pastor. Following marriage, I spent thirty-eight years in professional local church ministry service. I want to add here that second chair positions are different than first chair positions. While there is still a deep concern for the eternity of everyone under the influence of a second chair position, the overall weight of responsibility is significantly different between the first and second chair seats of leadership.

 As Steve described earlier, I do not have a call to professional ministry. I never had a Damascus Road experience. If I want, I can have a professional career outside the church, without feeling guilty, if I choose. I know this because if Steve were abducted by aliens tomorrow, I would not feel compelled to call the regional bishop for an appointment to a church or venture out on the itinerant evangelistic trail. I would not seek a minister to marry on the latest Christian dating service. I'm not principally opposed to remarrying a minister or to working in a professional role within a church setting, but I wouldn't feel compelled to. I currently take my divine holy assignment as a pastor's wife and helpmate very seriously. I also understand that as a Christian, I have a fundamental responsibility to work for the

The Uniqueness and Danger of Ministry

Lord, either through volunteering within my church or serving in another capacity. I'm not a consumer-taker without giving back.

However, divinely called to professional ministry or not, the minister's wife has a unique role and responsibility. I hope that after reading this chapter, the pastor's wife will realize she is not crazy, she is not alone, and there are practices she can put into place to combat burnout, loneliness, and dissatisfaction in serving, and find overall joy in life for herself and her family as they all serve in professional ministry.

This conversation is overdue, not only in my denomination but across every church denomination.[13] It is time to speak out and bring to light the uniqueness and danger of ministry for the minister's family, and even more specifically, the pastor's wife.

In any job or career, having a clear vision of success is essential. Defining success clearly is a key leadership practice, especially based on a job description. Does your church manual include a job description for the pastor's wife? Have you ever seen one? I certainly haven't. How does a pastor's wife know if she's doing a good job? If her role isn't clearly defined, each congregant may set their own unrealistic expectations, leading to ongoing frustration for the pastor's wife and disappointment for the congregation. Therefore, if the pastor and his wife do not create a realistic, proactive job description for the pastor's wife, typical default expectations tend to form.

Minister's wife job description: Must always appear happy, consistently portraying confidence while displaying an even temperament. Have the ability to empathize with others. Must be able to handle scrutiny of the public eye on a 24/7 basis, even when the scrutiny focuses on private situations. Excellent at resolving conflicts to ensure everyone's satisfaction. Patient, even in a crisis. Avoid challenging others when they are wrong and be ready to apologize, even if it's not your fault. Must appear experienced. Willing to keep paying endless dues. Striving to win people's approval repeatedly. Must develop thick skin yet retain a soft heart, able to resist offense and respond graciously when someone is negative about her husband or kids. Can handle not being liked by everyone. An effective communicator. Can retain joy in potentially toxic environments. Does not complain, at least in public. Last but not least, she is willing to stay the course and see it through to the end.[14]

---

13. Drumm, "Love Everybody."
14. Harvey, "What's Left."

Does this description resonate with any of you who are ministers' wives? Well, this is my paraphrase of an article about the job description for a politician's wife. As I read the article, the unreal similarities became clear. The intense scrutiny of the politician's wife and the pastor's wife is especially similar. For example, I had a lady walk up to me in the choir room before we entered the sanctuary, saying, "My sister and I were talking, and we liked the hairstyle you had before this one." Even my hair didn't escape judgment. Who would have thought my hairstyle would be a measure of success?

With this kind of job description, it's no wonder Dr. Sam Chand says, "The loneliest person on the face of the planet is the minister's spouse."[15] Let me press a little more into the loneliness piece, considering it's the number one challenge of pastors' wives.

A common reason for this loneliness is that the pastor's wife often lacks someone to discuss the unique challenges and dangers of ministry that she encounters. Just try explaining to someone the role/job description of a minister's wife who has never been in ministry leadership or lived it day-to-day. I tried a few times, and they could never understand the weight. I stopped trying.

Often, a minister's wife will keep her struggles to herself and chalk it up to carrying her cross because she doesn't want to appear weak to the congregation or other church leaders. She doesn't want to appear spiritually immature. She doesn't want her congregation to feel unsafe in their leadership. She doesn't want to cause any problems for her husband's ministry.

This anxiety-provoking scrutiny and appearance management posture can create what I call the "beach ball effect."

Imagine being in a swimming pool trying to hold a beach ball underwater. You may be able to do it for a while, but if there is any agitation in the pool, or you become tired or unbalanced in any way, that beach ball will explode. The pressure always wins because you'll never be stronger than the pressure, and you can never maintain perfect balance at all times. This unspoken expectation of suppression, never being able to express the weight of professional ministry to anyone, is exhausting. Suppressing the pressure of professional ministry for the minister or the minister's spouse is a high-stakes reality. The results can be depression, feeling hopeless, toxic loneliness, resentment, moral compromise, anger, disconnection, and

---

15. Sam Chand at the Church of God Top 200 conference, Atlanta, Georgia, 2018.

dissonance. Here are a couple of examples of real-life ministry from my experience.

During one of our youth pastorates, I attempted to connect with the pastor's wife, but by the time we were hired on staff, she had already burned out, becoming defensive and allowing only her family in. She was unavailable to me.

Another pastor's wife and friend had such negative experiences that she disconnected completely. She never went to church. The pastor and the kids went without her. Others have told me that they put on the professional ministry mask before leaving their homes every Sunday morning. Of course, these are anecdotal stories from individuals in the field of professional ministry, yet the research supports their accuracy.

> In observing pastors' wives in clinical interviews, workshops, retreats, and support groups, we have found frequent complaints concerning the many additional roles and high standards of role performance expected of them. These demands are often further compounded by the high visibility and accessibility of the pastorate. The high performance expectations placed upon them by congregations and church officials, as well as their self-imposed high expectations and lack of clarity regarding specific role expectations, result in reduced quality of life for many women married to clergy. This state of expectation is frequently evidenced by self-reported confusion, tension, and emotional stress and by the high incidence of burnout and loneliness observed by others.[16]

At this seemingly dark part of the chapter, don't forget that the pastor's wife is not only the most unique and dangerous vocation, but certainly has unique and exhilarating mountaintop experiences, too. I can honestly declare that the greatest joys in vocational life happen in ministry. What other job can claim as part of their work leading people/children to Christ—securing eternity and giving hurting people a chance to experience God by being heard, and serving as a sounding board for those who do not feel valued? Preparing meals for the sick helps alleviate their daily burden. Professional ministry is chock-full of the most diverse and positive experiences of any vocation I know. I can confidently say that there is nothing more rewarding than watching lives being transformed day to day in holistic ways.

Furthermore, pastors' wives can use their God-given gifts to serve in various capacities, such as music, teaching, business/finances, counseling,

---

16. Baker, "Predictors of Well-Being," 33.

intercessory prayer, and hospitality, among others. Consider the celebrations in the context of professional ministry. Ministers and their spouses share in the most diverse and best moments of life for members of the congregation, including weddings, anniversaries, job promotions, and much more.

Pastor's wife, please listen to me. Collaborate with your husband to proactively develop a clear, realistic job description for your role as the pastor's wife and ensure that church leadership and the congregation understand the criteria for your success. You can include it in the church manual if you'd like. The following are principles for my own job description that I've negotiated during my thirty-eight years of professional ministry. Use these principles to guide the creation of your own job description for the role of pastor's wife. Pay particular attention to the contrast between unrealistic and realistic expectations for the role of pastor's wife.

My presupposition for the role of the pastor's wife is based on gifting: identify your God-given gifts and decide in advance how you want to use them. Often, pastors' wives fill in gaps. When volunteers don't show up or a new program is needed, they frequently step into roles where they may not be naturally gifted or comfortable. Decide if you are willing to fill these gaps. If so, consider setting a time limit. Remember, you are not the savior of the ministry; the Lord is. He will provide, or he won't. He is sovereign.

> Unrealistic: *Must always appear happy, consistently portraying confidence while displaying an even temperament.*

While we are called to be Christlike in every situation, whether in a crisis or even around a complainer, wanting to be liked by everyone is an unrealistic goal. Congregations consist of many personalities, educational backgrounds, cultures, and financial statuses, each with its own set of expectations. Unless you have a PhD in clinical psychology and can assess all these traits instantly, you will misunderstand others and be misunderstood yourself. Recognizing and accepting that you cannot please everyone can be very freeing. The goal is to seek to hear God's approval above all else. He is our judge, not the congregation.

> Realistic: *Live authentically through life's ups and downs, consistently showing confidence in Christ while gradually developing a Christlike temperament.*

> Unrealistic: *Have the ability to empathize with others.*

The Uniqueness and Danger of Ministry

Empathy, the ability to understand and share others' feelings, is an innate gift that can be challenging to develop as a skill. However, we are called to show compassion toward others, which involves caring about their suffering or misfortunes. A pastor's wife will interact with many people who are hurting. She may not always understand or be able to empathize, but she is called to be compassionate.

> Realistic: *To the best of my ability, I will laugh with those who laugh, cry with those who cry, rejoice with those who rejoice, and mourn with those who mourn.*

> Unrealistic: *Must be able to handle scrutiny of the public eye on a 24/7 basis, even when the scrutiny focuses on private situations.*

Being in the public eye of the congregation and community is unavoidable; it is an inherent part of ministry. More than the typical family, the ministry family is viewed through a magnifying glass, revealing all manner of imperfections. This should not lead to a pursuit of perfection or resentment of reality. Instead, let awareness of the scrutiny inherent in professional ministry provide wisdom for public life. Also, avoid emphasizing this reality to your children by constantly reminding them of it. The only scrutiny you should highlight regarding your children's public life is the Holy Spirit's assessment of Christlike character. Honoring the Holy Spirit in every aspect of life is the only standard the ministry family should uphold. So, when one of your children shares a story about a church member pointing out that they are the pastor's kid and should know better, dismiss the church member and redirect the child to the Holy Spirit. If the Holy Spirit isn't displeased with the child's behavior, then what the church member thinks doesn't matter. I also believe the 24/7 rule of always being "on" should not apply to the pastor's family. Be sure to protect the privacy of the ministry family as much as possible. It's wise to let your children know that what happens in the pastor's home stays in the pastor's home. Pastor, this includes not using your wife or kids in sermon illustrations unless you have prior approval.

> Realistic: *Embraces the inherent reality of ministry life in the public eye without paranoia or undue concern beyond the scrutiny of the Holy Spirit. I will safeguard my children from excessive appearance*

management. To the best of my ability, I will create ample and safe space for my family to express themselves away from the public eye.

Unrealistic: *Excellent at resolving conflicts to ensure everyone's satisfaction.*

Resolving conflict is a risky, tedious challenge that, if not handled well, could cause serious harm to a church and a pastor's family. Unless a pastor's wife is trained in conflict management or counseling, it's essential for someone skilled in these areas to step in and mediate. A strategic plan for resolving conflict must be in place to ensure fairness and satisfaction with the outcome, and it should never be solely the responsibility of the pastor's wife.

Realistic: *Will be vigilant in identifying potential personal and church conflicts early and refer them to the appropriate leaders. Additionally, I will personally honor the covenantal nature of private before public biblical conflict resolution by going directly to the person involved to resolve the issue, preventing the devil from gaining a foothold.*

Unrealistic: *Patient, even in a crisis.*

Because the devil aims to devour and destroy, churches will inevitably face moments of crisis. Patience remains a vital virtue during these times. The pastor's wife will also confront crisis moments. She is human and must evaluate her own spiritual gifts and fruits of the Spirit during those times. If the fruit of patience isn't fully developed, she might need to step back and regroup. What helped me during crises was reminding myself that God sees what we cannot see and knows what we cannot know. He anticipated the crisis, is in the middle of it, and has already mapped out the outcome. The pastor's wife should never assume that resolving the crisis depends solely on her.

Realistic: *I will be as patient with myself as I attempt to be patient with others.*

The Uniqueness and Danger of Ministry

> Unrealistic: *Avoid challenging others when they are wrong and ready to apologize, even if it's not your fault.*

There are times when congregational leadership or paid staff challenge a pastoral decision. When this happens in ministry, it is often very personal and painful for the pastor's wife. Usually, the conflict involves someone the pastor's wife knows well and may even be friends with. I remember a specific crisis related to the youth pastor position. After some poor hiring decisions and numerous interviews, Steve was unsure how to fill the vacancy. One morning, he came to the breakfast table believing that God had revealed a plan to staff the position from within rather than from outside. At the regularly scheduled staff meeting, he shared the plan to reorganize several departments. The plan was strategic and multilayered. One staff member disagreed and strongly challenged it. When Steve and the staff member tried to resolve the disagreement, Steve eventually ended the discussion and asked the staff member to follow the leader—something they did passively, seemingly offended at not being heard. Often, when church leaders or staff express disagreement, they assume that the pastor and/or his wife didn't listen to them because, in their view, if the pastor or his wife had heard them, they would have recognized that the church leader or staff person was right. The reality is, the staff member was heard; Steve simply didn't agree. Steve's stance of disagreement was completely incomprehensible to the staff member, who believed they were so brilliant that any reasonable person would agree with them. It became clear that the staff member's trust in Steve's leadership had eroded due to the disagreement. Their passive support generalized to others, making Steve's leadership more difficult.

As it turned out, Steve's creative department shuffle to fill the youth pastor role didn't work out as he had hoped and became just another painful youth ministry transition. It was appropriate to challenge the staff pastor and insist they follow the leader. Furthermore, there was no need to apologize. Second chair leaders should actively support the first chair leader. If they can't, they need to own it and step aside rather than stay and sour. Sometimes, avoiding conflict may be, in rare cases, the right choice; and yes, sometimes we need to apologize, but it is not always necessary to avoid conflict.

> Realistic: *Will address church members when they are out of line and expect correction. If this creates the potential for offense, I will invite others into the mix. I will not take the fall for others or excuse*

> their bad behavior. I confidently expect to be challenged as well on my bad behavior, seeking the correction of the church family for my continued sanctification.

> Unrealistic: *Must appear experienced.*

Education and experience are crucial for performing a job well. If a pastor's wife wants to fill a role or position but lacks the necessary education or experience, she should be encouraged to work toward earning those qualifications. However, just because a position is available does not mean the pastor's wife is automatically the best person for the job.

> Realistic: *Will continually pursue to personally improve my ability to serve Christ and the church.*

> Unrealistic: *Willing to keep paying endless dues. Striving to win people's approval repeatedly.*

As a pastor's wife, I genuinely wanted the congregation to be proud of me. I never wanted to be a disappointment and aimed to serve them well. It was important to me that they trusted me. However, because of the wide range of emotional and spiritual maturity among the members, there were times—no matter how hard I tried—I would inevitably fall short of someone's expectations. Constantly seeking approval can lead to dissatisfaction and frustration in serving the Lord. The pastor's wife must accept that she will never please everyone in the congregation. Her main concern should be to please the one who truly matters: Jesus Christ. Furthermore, the pastor must keep reminding his wife that there are no dues, and striving for people's approval is like King Solomon's pursuit of wind.

> Realistic: *Will live by grace and grace alone. Will not pay dues to earn my keep in the church. Jesus paid my dues in full, there is nothing left to pay. Whereas I desire to live an attractive and likable life in Christ, I will not strive to win the approval of others, only the applause of God.*

The Uniqueness and Danger of Ministry

> Unrealistic: *Must develop thick skin yet retain a soft heart, able to resist offense and respond graciously when someone is negative about her husband or kids. Can handle not being liked by everyone.*

Maintaining a compassionate attitude toward members who are negative about her husband and/or children is likely the biggest challenge for the pastor's wife. Responding graciously to congregational complaints about the pastoral family is not easy. I've heard some say it takes a village to raise children. I've also learned that in every village, there are a number of idiots. Church members often appoint themselves as surrogate parents to the pastor's kids, even when they aren't invited. A pastor's wife must defend her family from unrealistic expectations placed on them. This can be done in a Christlike way, but she might need a mediator or witness to avoid being misquoted or misunderstood. Our family has been entrusted to us by God to protect and nurture. Pastor, you must support your wife on this issue.

> Realistic: *I will anchor my identity in Christ so deeply that I will be impervious to offense. However, when my husband or family is negatively discussed, I expect that the church leadership will support us, not dismissing a legitimate charge and correcting an illegitimate one.*

> Unrealistic: *An effective communicator.*

It is not always true that a pastor's wife feels comfortable being in the spotlight. She may not have the gift of preaching or teaching. Perhaps her strength lies in working behind the scenes or managing in the office. A pastor's wife should never be expected to perform beyond her talents. God has given her specific abilities according to his will for her life and her church.

> Realistic: *Will communicate as effectively as God has gifted me. This may be singing, writing, speaking, painting, or not at all in a public way.*

> Unrealistic: *Can retain joy in potentially toxic environments.*

Joy is different from happiness. Our happiness depends on our circumstances, but joy comes from our relationship with Christ. When toxic situations arise—and they will—the pastor's wife must heavily rely on her

The Wisdom of Ministerial Family Soul Health

relationship with Jesus to keep her joy alive. She should also gather a group of covenant sisters with whom she can cuss, pray, and laugh. (Note: for those who choked on the word "cuss" in the previous sentence, think of it as "vent." Relax, it's just that the word "cuss" captures the emotion of venting better than simply saying "vent.")

> Realistic: *Will actively address toxic situations by emphasizing biblical principles of Christian harmony. Also, I will maintain covenantal relationships outside the church that keep me accountable and encouraged.*

> Unrealistic: *Does not complain, at least in public.*

Complaining and critical thinking are two very different things, especially when it comes to tone. Every pastor should want his wife to help him think critically. This is very different from complaining. Complaining typically comes without solutions. However, critical thinking always results in creative solutions.

> Realistic: *Seeks and provides honest evaluations of oneself and the ministry.*

> Unrealistic: *Last but not least, they are willing to stay the course and see it through to the end.*

A minister who has experienced a Damascus Road calling to preach the gospel, like Paul, bears the weight and burden of eternity for the congregation on his shoulders. The pastor's wife helps balance that weight in every way. She may not have a calling to ministry herself, but she is definitely on a holy assignment. Because their calling and holy assignment affect eternity for those they shepherd, the devil's goal is to get them to quit. The goal of this book is to encourage the pastor and his family to stay the course and finish the race so they hear "well done" from the master.

> Realistic: *Will be alert to the possibility that leaving a ministry context might be better than staying. This should be done in the safety of many wise counselors.*

The Uniqueness and Danger of Ministry

The principles outlined for a pastor's wife job description are meant to help you create your own. Once you have a clear idea of what a good role as a pastor's wife entails, it's important to review and evaluate yourself in consultation with your husband and trusted friends. Remember to schedule this biannual reflection in your calendar.

The churches we've served have contained a rich diversity of precious people who have made indelible positive contributions to our lives. I wouldn't trade those people or experiences of church love and unity for any other life outside of ministry. I'm glad Steve was divinely redirected away from medicine and toward ministry (well, it would have been nice if the money had been comparable, but I digress). The joy of ministry is real, albeit the bother remains. We all love the mountaintop experiences of ministry. Still, the truth is that these experiences, wonderful as they are, comprise only about 20 percent of ministry, in my experience and according to research.

What about the other 80 percent? What about the challenges and stressors that weigh heavily on the pastor and his wife? In this way, being the wife of a minister is so different than being the wife of a doctor, accountant, teacher, truck driver, or inventory specialist. What doctors' wives feel the pain of the patients? What plumber's wife worries about the flooded basement of a client? What accountant's wife expects on Sunday or at a social event to see a client who just filed bankruptcy, losing everything? Yet, the pastor's wife bears the weight of souls entrusted to her husband's ministry with equal love. Professional ministry holds a unique and dangerous diversity and depth of experience for the spouse and family of a professional minister. Steve calls them extreme soul swings.

Pastors of non-Damascus Road–called wives, put this book down and hug your wife, thanking her for anchoring her life's calling in yours just because she loved you enough to marry you. Do it, right now. I'll wait.

OK, onward.

Enough of me telling my story. Check out the following stories from an informal survey I conducted with dozens of pastors' wives and children. I know that there are an equal number of mountaintop stories, but they get front page press. These stories are the ones buried in the back pages. Today I'm bringing them to the front.

The Wisdom of Ministerial Family Soul Health

Washington State

"It hurts when seasoned people who you have been involved with and have poured yourself into leave the church. After walking with them through very dark valleys, they decide to attend a church down the street. It is a double stinger when they don't even tell you goodbye or give a reason. Very awkward when you see them in town and they act all chummy."

Ohio

"I want to quit! Ministry has been extremely hard. I am praying God will help me regain the sweetness that I once had. I am fighting bitterness and trying to keep Christ in focus."

Georgia

"My greatest struggle is burnout. I am just so tired."

Alabama

"My greatest struggle is knowing who I can trust. Your words or struggles can be used against you. It can be very lonely."

Indiana

"The most difficult for me is when my husband, the pastor, has to make a difficult or controversial decision and then watch him being attacked personally. I also struggle watching my kids being affected adversely by the church just because they are the pastor's kids. I don't want them to be turned off to the church due to the cruelty of the people."

California

"It is difficult when we work so hard for God, being obedient, and then being hurt unjustifiably and mistreated by the flock. The pain and scars from the hurtful words and attacks on the pastor are real. It affects him, me, and the kids. These episodes can be devastating and life-changing."

The Uniqueness and Danger of Ministry

Florida

"Feelings of loneliness can creep up on me at the most unexpected times. For instance, I organize two ladies' Bible studies. I visit each table weekly to engage in discussions with all the ladies. Inevitably, I'll have one or two table leaders make comments about how nervous they are because I sat there. Since I work so hard at being real and transparent and 'just me', situations similar to this can make me feel like some women can't push past my leader role and see me as just one of them."

Florida

"Busyness is my biggest struggle and can affect my relationship with God. Without him, I cannot do this job. Our busy schedules (at church and in life) can steal time with him if I let it. So, I have to fight to maintain my personal and intimate time with God."

Iowa

"It is challenging when people volunteer to fill a void and then do not show up. The task often falls to me, and I already have too many other responsibilities. But someone has to fill the void."

Retired pastor's wife in Florida

"Tap dancing and juggling for the adoration of the people we are to serve. We become disingenuous and start wearing a mask. We deny our fatigue, our frustrations, and our faults in pursuit of a non-existent image. We can lose our souls in this dreadful pride."

Florida PK

"A PK is in the spotlight. If the church kids get into trouble, the PK is usually blamed. A PK is expected to be perfect and serve as an example. As soon as people know you are a PK, they automatically expect or assume the PK is perfect or wild."

The Wisdom of Ministerial Family Soul Health

California PK

"I remember loneliness being my mom's greatest struggle. Trusting women in the church was difficult. Developing deep relationships was a challenge. For me, as a PK, kids tend to follow the patterns they have set before them. Trusting other women in church became my difficulty. Also, seeing my father as a target many times was difficult, especially when I saw how hard he worked and how deeply he loved the people."

Tennessee PK—trapped

"A lady from church invited me to her home for a 'ladies' dinner.' I was the first to arrive, so I greeted others who strangely handed me wrapped gifts as they entered. I said I was not aware we were to bring gifts. The hostess said, 'No, these gifts are for you.' I jokingly asked, 'Am I dying?' We laughed. At their insistence, I opened all the gifts. Only five ladies had arrived, so I asked where everyone else was. Just us, the hostess said, 'We thought it would be more intimate to speak about some things.' The ladies started chatting about church. I finally asked, 'What exactly is this about?' One lady said, 'Frankly, we are tired of your DAD! For God's sake, why don't you buy him a hearing aid? We're also fed up with brother "so and so" being in charge of the adult Sunday school. He isn't even Spirit-filled. He can't talk in tongues like us.'

"I calmly stood up and asked the lady, who was the church clerk, why she would let me fall prey and walk into this. She was supposed to help guard the church and was closest to the pastor. As I exited, I threw the gifts into the kitchen trash can.

"My car had been blocked in, and the only route out was through the pretty white picket fence and over the meticulously manicured flower garden. My car dragged that white picket fence quite a distance down the road before dislodging. I am pretty sure the deep ruts I left in the flower garden will need a lot of attention.

"The next day was Sunday. We were all in church together. One lady on the piano bench, the others in the pews as I sang, led the choir, and ran the sound."

These stories are just a small sampling from my survey. I understand that any of these stories could be contextualized in a non-ministry setting, such as a department store or accounting firm. We might even expect stories like that in a "secular" environment, but in church with brothers and sisters in Christ, it's just so much more painful and incongruent from what it's supposed to be. The unrealistically high expectations, pressure, and scrutiny intrinsic to being the pastor's wife and children are ineffable.

Recently, Steve invited a local church pastor to speak in his pastoral ministries class. Steve said he did an excellent job explaining the ministry to the students. Interestingly, one of his remarks to the students was, "Your wife/spouse will make or break your ministry." I was not surprised to hear this, as I have heard this many times before. The minister's spouse not only has the job description to live up to within the congregation, but now she also has the added pressure of making or breaking her husband's ministry career.

How many engineers, accountants, plumbers, etc. would say the same thing? Do plumbers worry that their spouse will make or break their plumbing career? Goodness, the pressure to perform.

Speaking of performance. How many middle managers' spouses have to be interviewed to see if their husbands would receive a promotion? Crazy, right? I've had to be interviewed by a board of ministers for my husband to advance in ministry. One board member said, "Your husband is a handsome man. There will be other women in the churches where you serve who will pursue him. Are you prepared to meet his sexual needs to avoid him being lured away?" I was shocked, surprised, and embarrassed by his question. I fumbled around for a couple of seconds, then regained my composure and courage. I looked him square in the eyes and said, "Well, I guess I'd better step it up a notch."

Does this happen in any other profession? My husband loved my response and wanted to print "Step it up a notch!" T-shirts for pastors' wives, but that's not the point. Anyway. Goodness, pastor's wives can't make this stuff up.

Alrighty, let me shift gears here and offer several practical nuggets of wisdom from my over sixty years of ministry for protecting yourself and your family.

Nugget One: Maintain proper priorities with impenetrable boundaries.

In my mind, this is the only priority order: God, family, church. I cannot even count the times I have heard pastors' kids say that they believe church was more important to their parents than they were. Be clear, the church is last on the list of priorities.

The definition of an impenetrable boundary is a barrier that is impossible to pass through. Set impenetrable boundaries around things that you would die for. Let me list some that our family, over the years, has identified as impenetrable boundaries:

- **The sanctity of your marriage.** This means that you and your husband must establish boundaries that protect your marital integrity mutually—for instance, not meeting online or in person alone with someone of the opposite gender. Jointly owning social media accounts, sharing a calendar, and turning on location service on your phone will reveal your location at all times to your spouse.

- **The sanctity of your home.** Even if a church parsonage. Courageously create a culture of respect for the privacy of your family, even though your husband has a very public position. In a church context, often state that your home is a place of warmth and welcome, but only when you're invited. Ask your people to please not drop in unannounced. Your home is a personal sanctuary for you and your family—a place where you can let down your guard. Where unconditional love prevails, it is a place to create positive lifelong memories with and for your spouse and children. A place to refresh and renew. A place for healing. So, protect your home.

- **The sanctity of kids' events.** School events, sports within reason, recitals, or competitions are more important than church events. You respect the boundaries of the church and expect its members to respect yours. Establishing this boundary will require you and your minister husband to coordinate the family and church calendar. Have the courage to say "That church event won't happen on that day and time," or "That church event can happen on that day and time, but without the pastor and family."

- **The sanctity of meals.** The communion meal in the New Testament is called a meal because food is something that everyone must have, and we can leverage that meal with loving union among those who share in it. Maybe it's dinner at 5:00 p.m. always. Or breakfast before school. Or a meal at the grandparents' house every Sunday. Or all three. Make at least one meal a day or week with your immediate

- **The secularity of technology.** As I mentioned, I grew up in a pastor's home. My mom planned a family meal every day after I returned from school. She took the phones off the hook so no one could call in. She locked the doors and requested that no one answer if someone came knocking. This routine describes our family meal time. As a little girl, this message told me that I was more important than any phone call or uninvited visitor. I have spoken to many adult PKs who have said that when they were children, they always thought the church was more important than they were.

The most important takeaway of this wisdom is this: You and your pastor/husband are the chief evangelist and disciple maker of your children. You can work so hard to win the whole world (your church) that you can lose your children in the process. Don't be that family.

However, let's be genuine and honest. You can do everything right, and your children can still choose to run off into a ditch. We, at least, do the best we can. When at a loss, seek wise counsel outside yourselves for your children's sake. Remember, maintain proper priorities with impenetrable boundaries.

Nugget Two: Self-love is good love.

The ministry includes you. The church is expecting you to pour into them, and you can't pour from an empty cup. You need "you time!" What rejuvenates you, refreshes you, and gives you energy? Steve's teachings on the principle of a pipeline or reservoir soul, along with the practices of Sabbath and renewal zones mentioned previously, are critical for this nugget of wisdom. Make sure you have a life beyond church. Join a fun band unrelated to church. Engage in an activity that is entirely unrelated to church programs or people. Train in art, archery, martial arts, information technology, cooking, farming, horseback riding, poetry, and anything that generates enthusiasm and energy. If at all possible, do something like I've suggested with your spouse or as a family.

Another dimension of self-love is the oneness you share with your husband. Christian marriage is centrally a miracle of two becoming one. Your holistic health includes your marital health. Commit to being on the same page. Not divided. Remember, the kids grow up and move on. The congregation has its own best interests at heart. You know you've had church members who you and your husband served and loved for many years who leave to attend the church down the street, without even saying goodbye, ghosting you. Also, your church denomination will carry on with or without you. One day, it will be only you and your husband. Nurture your relationship so you will still have each other when you empty the nest and step back from professional ministry leadership.

Create opportunities for each other to feel special. Show affection often and in front of the kids (within reason, of course; unless, like Steve, you just want to gross them out). Attentiveness is the foundational expression of love. Cultivate attentiveness. This lived example of attentiveness and affection is great modeling for your children's future relationships. Affirm each other, privately and publicly. Protect each other at all costs. Establish a unified front and have each other's back. Go on marriage retreats, not a retreat that you are leading. Ask each other, often, how you can love and serve the other better. Do not allow the ministry to become a mistress to your husband or you. Develop a relationship with a good Christian marriage and family counselor for quarterly relational sanity checks. This extra-church relationship is just good marital health and hygiene practice.

Nugget Three: Pray for covenant sisters.

Like every David needs a Jonathan, every Naomi needs a Ruth. "Faithful are the wounds of a friend: profuse are the kisses of an enemy. Wounds from a sincere friend are better than man's kisses from an enemy."

—PROVERBS 27:6

In 2012, I found myself feeling alone as I navigated ministry difficulties. I could not and would not confide in any staff wife because my husband was their husband's boss. I would not confide in a congregant; I didn't want them to carry any of the weight, and they wouldn't understand anyway. I needed like-minded sisters, pastors' wives, who understood. I wanted to connect with women who could walk alongside me, and I could walk alongside them in our pastor's wife journey. I began praying for the Lord to direct me. He inspired me to start a pastors' wives retreat. So, I started praying, "Who, Lord, would you have me invite on this retreat?" It took me a year to put it all together. I wanted it to be a time of worship, healing, fun, and bonding. I prayed about who I would choose. I prayed for the Lord to put the right women in my path. The guidelines for selecting these retreat sisters were as follows. They had to be a part of my history. We had to have something in common. They had to be lead pastors' wives.

Over that year, the Lord allowed me to cross paths with longtime friends whom I had not seen or talked with in years. When I would reconnect with these friends, the Lord would just touch my heart and say to me, "Invite her." Two of the women chosen were constant contact friends. So after a year, the retreat became a reality.

This retreat was made up of me and five friends. These sisters became my life raft, or lifeline, if you will. In the first five years, we gathered twice a year. Soon, elderly parents were in need, and grandchildren became a part of our world. We had to reduce our meetings to one a year. We would spend four days praying for each other, our families, our children, and our grandchildren. We shared our burdens and carried each other's burdens. We shared ministry ideas for events and women's ministry plans. We prayed for our husbands and their calling. We prayed for our personal ministries and personal walks with Jesus. We witnessed miracles happening in all these areas we prayed about.

I encourage all pastors' wives to form a pastors' wives sisters group that you can meet with regularly. Maybe you want to start with one or two others and build from there, or not. It will change your life for the better. We need each other. You can't be yourself by yourself!

Nugget Four: Soul health planning (SHP) is nonnegotiable.

Make this an annual family practice. Each fall, begin scheduling time to get alone with the Holy Spirit to listen for direction regarding next year's SHP. Encourage your kids to do the same. This kind of atypical planning will take training, tenacity, and time to get traction. But once traction happens and soul health planning and sharing become a standard operating procedure of your family, the generational soul health benefits will be many.

It took some time, but our family now looks forward to curating and sharing our annual SHPs each New Year's Eve. It's become a tradition. Some join online, while others attend in person, where we take turns sharing what the Holy Spirit has forecasted for our soul health in the following year. Our

The Wisdom of Ministerial Family Soul Health

nest is empty now, yet our adult kids and, slowly but surely, their kids are making soul health planning an annual nonnegotiable.

In case you missed it, Steve provides a detailed section above concerning soul health planning, and there are lots of SHP resources in appendix 2.

OK, final nugget of wisdom. It's more like a demand.

Pastor's wife, demand, and I mean demand, that the minister you are married to pastor you and your family better than they pastor the church. You should feel more pastored than the church members do by your husband. Ministry is unique and dangerous. Ministry can be lonely. Demand that your minister husband take the lead, with your support and input, to establish preventative practices of soul health and hygiene to safeguard your soul and the souls of your family against the intrinsic uniqueness and danger of ministry. Demand that more creative thought and energy be invested in this soul health family programming than is currently applied to the church. Those practices at a bare minimum must include the following.

- Maintaining proper priorities with impenetrable boundaries regarding:
  - The sanctity of your marriage
  - The sanctity of your home
  - The sanctity of events for your kids
  - Nonnegotiable annual soul health planning

Furthermore, demand that your minister husband support you in the following.

- Maintaining proper priorities with impenetrable boundaries for yourself regarding:
  - Self-love is good love
  - Covenant sisters
  - Personal soul health planning

We all know professional ministry is not for the faint of heart. The pastor's wife's role may resemble that of a circus performer, taming lions and keeping multiple life responsibility plates spinning in the air at the same time. She may work a job outside the home to help provide financially for her family. She serves as the pastor's helpmate, working to fill in the gaps of church ministry, typically without monetary compensation, yet with all the expectations of a paid worker. She seeks to provide and maintain a haven in her home for her family. Protecting her kids and raising them to love God and the church is a priority. She has all these typical plates spinning, but with one critical addition: like Paul, concern for God's eternal church. Do not underestimate the often unconscious weight of this intrinsic burden of professional ministry. My prayer is that the pastor's wife will find and maintain joy and satisfaction in her role and realize she is not crazy or alone on her journey.

5

The *Wrap-Up* of Ministerial Soul Health

A Complete Soul Transmission

In the first four chapters, I've covered the ***Why***, ***What***, ***Work***, and ***Wisdom*** of ministerial soul health. Now for the ***Wrap-Up***. As a preacher, I needed an alliteration: the 5 Ws.

REGARDLESS OF CONTEXT, OUR souls are being formed from the moment of conception. Our sense of safety, confidence, security, attachments, fun, language, God, family, marriage, nationality, socioeconomic status, friendship, and so on are all being formed in a 360-degree kind of formation. From the music our parents listen to, the sports our family values or supports, to the food we like or dislike and the way we worship, everything about us is being shaped by the contextual water we swim in.

Remember that fish story where the old fish was swimming along and saw a couple of young fish swimming toward her in the opposite direction, so she extended hospitality by asking, "How's the water, boys?" To which the young fish just looked incredulously at the old fish and swam by. Later, one of the young fish said to the other young fish, "What's water?"

Yeah, we're the young fish. The contextual cultural water is forming us; we're born in it and swim in it our entire life on earth. To the point where we don't even notice how much things like the 24/7 news cycle are shaping our souls as they drone in the background. Spiritual formation is the process of awakening to find ourselves immersed in this cultural current, then slowly and strategically turning our souls around to swim against the kingdom of the world current. Spiritual formation is an invitation to follow the old fish: yes, in the world but not of the world. But the rip current of worldly culture has conveyed us along for so long, we're way out to sea, so to speak. To swim in this new direction will require intentional, strategic, and diligent soul training. Even as a Christian, we have a lot of soul re-training and re-forming to do in partnership with God.

I love how evangelical Pentecostal pastor Rich Villodas describes the challenge of spiritual formation in this cultural moment of speed as king: "What I've learned has reinforced the truth that unless we live with an intentional commitment to slow down, we have no hope for a quality of life that allows Jesus to form us into his image."[1] Did you hear that? "No hope" for Christlike formation unless we change direction and speed.

How we think, feel, and respond to stimuli has been conditioned unconsciously by the constant input and output of our external and internal context. This formation is the result of a slow and lengthy process. You are who you are because your context has formed you into who you are. But is who you are who you were created to be? Without Christ, and often with Christ, we are perceptibly and imperceptibly being formed. Without Christ, we are conditioned by the world. With Christ, we are reconditioned by the Spirit. This reconditioning is sanctification. Or in other words, spiritual formation.

Although the notion of spiritual formation is another way of saying discipleship, apprenticeship, soul health, or sanctification, for many evangelicals, it's a fringe, weird Christian mysticism that needs demystification. Spiritual formation, as a formal process of soul health, is often associated with ancient monasticism or Catholicism. Although not inaccurate, this description does not provide a complete picture of the formal sanctifying process, commonly referred to as spiritual formation, in our contemporary vernacular.

The following comment resonates so viscerally with me. I don't know exactly where I heard it, but it was attributed to theologian Ronald Rolheiser: "Theology is the rules of the game, spiritual formation is the game."[2]

---

1. Villodas, *Deeply Formed Life*, 9.
2. If you haven't read Rolheiser's little book *Domestic Monastery*, you're cheating

The Wrap-Up of Ministerial Soul Health

For the Christian message to be coherent in this cultural moment, we Christian ministers have got to integrate great thinking with great living. Spiritual formation is a rich process for this integration.

If you are interested in soul health, the most robust way I know of to engage with the process is to explore the Gospel-centered, orthodox, morally convictional, holistic, slow, intentional, disciplined life of sanctifying spiritual formation. Therefore, consider the following an invitation to Baptists, Pentecostals, Methodists, Catholics, nondenominationalists, or contemplatives to soften your focus and see with your soul that which you haven't previously seen.

I know, I'm gonna use another preacher tactic here, an illustration. Go with me. My first mission trip was to the Caribbean island of Antigua. On the free day, we took the team to the beach, where snorkeling was an option. I'd never snorkeled before and felt apprehensive about the unknown elements of the experience. But I agreed to follow Brother Lee into the gorgeous Caribbean water to Long Reef. When we arrived at one end of Long Reef, Brother Lee instructed me to follow the reef to the other end. He said that when I do this, I would be amazed by what I saw. So, I fitted my mask and snorkel, dropped below the surface, and anxiously sped down the reef to the other end. When I rose from under the water, I was very disappointed. The reef appeared barren to me. I hardly saw anything except bland coral and a few colorful darting fish. I revealed this to Brother Lee. He wasn't surprised. With kindness, he patiently asked me to pass the reef once more, but this time, slowing to almost a drifting float and softening my focus so I could see what I missed.

Surprised at his response, and a little offended, I accepted the renewed and reframed invitation. I again fitted my mask and snorkel, then dropped below the surface where he gently held my hand as we drifted, not swam, but drifted slowly the length of Long Reef. It was unbelievable. I can confidently say that snorkel crack hit my brain, and I was hooked. What I missed due to my defensive posture and speed of passing over the reef was that every millimeter of the reef was bursting with life and color. Although I did snorkel the reef and thought I had seen all there was to see, I missed 95 percent of its richness of life.

Going forward, I'm inviting you to join me in a softened focus and slow pass over the richness of the spiritual formation reef. You may have

---

yourself. It's a great read on the practical application of spiritual formation in everyday life.

passed by or over spiritual formation before, but perhaps you never got close enough. Maybe you passed over it too fast, or with a poor guide. Hear me, please; God's speed is *slow*! He is never in a hurry for you to learn anything or become something. He is outside time. You can't hurry up and become like Christ. Just relax, soften your focus, slow your soul, take my hand, and let me pass you over the richness of spiritual formation or soul health, as I'm calling this reef, so to speak.

Starting with a couple of orienting definitions of spiritual formation may help warm you up to the demystifying process. Soften your focus and take in the following definitions, imagining those providing the definitions are simply discussing sanctification or discipleship in a different, yet, in my opinion, more coherent and comprehensive way:

> Christian spiritual formation is the intentional engagement of practices that open one's soul to the transforming work of the Holy Spirit to make one more like Christ for the sake of others.[3]

> An interactive process by which God the Father fashions believers into the image of his Son, Jesus, through the empowerment of the Holy Spirit by fostering development in seven primary life dimensions (spirit, emotions, relationships, intellect, vocation, physical health, and resource stewardship).[4]

Unless you're just theologically pugnacious, these are tough to argue with in any rational way. Furthermore, you might be wondering how these definitions are different from your definition of discipleship, or Bible study, or Sunday school. I agree; spiritual formation is not entirely distinct from what you may know as discipleship or Sunday school. Hang with me here. The key is that during the twentieth century, these familiar programs like discipleship and Sunday school were oriented to education, or information. The difference is that spiritual formation invites the participant to see beyond impersonal information to personal transformation. For spiritual formation, the goal is to operationalize information about Christianity into everyday life routines or habits that re-form ourselves holistically over time into Christians. So, from definitions like this, I cobbled together the following to help me envision a practical, holistic approach to soul sanctification as a spiritual formation hermeneutic.

---

3. Mulholland, *Invitation to a Journey*, 146.
4. Chandler, *Christian Spiritual Formation*, 12.

The Wrap-Up of Ministerial Soul Health

My life goal is to nurture a love for God, expressed by loving others as I love myself and keeping constant company with Jesus (Matt 11, 22). Therefore, I think of myself as an apprentice of Jesus Christ (Christopraxis, Gal 4:19, 2 Cor 5:13–21). Intentionally conditioning my soul to be like him in every way (Christoforming, Eph 4:13) so that all who experience me will continue to experience the incarnation of Christ (incarnational, Acts 1:8, John 14:9).

For the sake of clarity:

- Christoforming: Being like Christ was in character
- Christopraxis: Doing what Christ did and taught
- Incarnational: Living like Christ lived as his light in the world

Use the definitions and my personal life hermeneutic as raw material to craft your definition of spiritual formation or life hermeneutic. You can surely adapt the content above to your particular place on the spectrum of Christian faith traditions. Yep, we're all on the spectrum.

My life and ministry history include experience and education in both the charismatic and contemplative traditions. Generally, my experience is that most others and I live at one or the other of these seemingly opposite ends of the Christian faith traditions spectrum. Or perhaps you're somewhere on the spectrum in between leaning to one end or the other. What if this faith tradition spectrum or chasm could be easily bridged by simply dropping our arrogance? Yes, arrogance. Charismatics, contemplatives, and many in between often become entrenched in the arrogance of their tradition's supremacy. This arrogance is the result of hyper-focus. It's the kind of focus I had when I first passed over the reef, which closed my eyes to its richness, assuming I was seeing all there was to see.

What if the kingdom of God here is not an either-or, but a both-and? What if this spectrum of siloed extremes, hyper-focus, and defensiveness is what's closing our eyes to the richness of wise integration? What if embracing the diversity of earth and the unity of heaven reveals the life and life more abundantly that Jesus spoke of? Where God's will is done on earth as it is in heaven. What if we're better together than apart? What if there is an answer to the prayer Jesus prayed in John 17, for us to become one with him and each other?

I think it would be helpful for this charismatic/Pentecostal to riff on his contemplative integration as a means of invitation for you to consider something similar. With that caveat, I offer this oxymoron to you, the "charismatic contemplative." Oil and water, I know. So, let me offer another illustration that could help you relax and open your soul to the opposite end of the faith tradition spectrum, or at least a neighboring faith tradition on the spectrum. The motivation behind sharing this alternative illustration is to offer a vision of a soul that slows us and softens our focus, allowing us to see what riches might be added to our soul by ideas and practices from someone else's soul.

Imagine the soul as a transmission. In a transmission, there is a full range of gears from slow to fast. For a vehicle to advance, it requires a full complement of gears. A transmission with only slow gears would not serve the driver very well. And of course, a transmission would not serve the driver very well either with only fast gears. Imagine a place where the fast and loud coexist in harmony with the slow and quiet. Can you imagine a fully geared soul?[5]

In this chapter, I'm offering a way to add gears, so to speak, to your soul transmission, to help you advance on the road to Christlikeness. To do this, I need to survey the history of spiritual formation briefly, or as I'm calling it, soul health.

Consider the genesis of the spiritual formation movement with Jesus. A movement away from the legalism of pharisaical law toward freedom in grace. He loved to be at parties (think: the wedding at Cana or Matthew's and Zacchaeus's houses) and with people (think: his disciples or the large crowds that he would gather). However, as a counterbalance, he also loved to be alone and quiet, to retreat, and to spend time with only a few (think: how he often withdrew to the wilderness from the crowds or only asked Peter, James, and John to hang out). Jesus loved the crowds (think: Sermon on the Mount or feeding the five thousand) and also following the Spirit alone into the desert (think: how he sent the crowds away and his temptations in the desert). In Jesus, we see the full complement of both charismatic and contemplative gears with everything in between. Balance and integration are the centerpiece in the spiritually formative life of Jesus Christ, modeled for all those who follow him. This balance and integration was his way, the Way as it would come to be known. As his name suggests, Jesus Christ is the incarnational embodiment of both the charismatic and contemplative ends of the soul spectrum and everything in between. Jesus is the divine example of a soul transmission with a full range of gears. Listen to how

---

5. Check out *The Charismatic Contemplative Podcast* in appendix 1 under Resources for a deeper dive.

The Wrap-Up of Ministerial Soul Health

Richard Foster puts the life of Jesus as holistic sacramental living: "This way of sacramental living calls out to us. It calls us to make all our waking and sleeping, all our working and playing, all our living and loving flow out from the divine wellspring. It can; Jesus points the way."[6]

In Christ is the fullness of everything humans were created to be. The joy of soul health is realizing in real time the actualization of Christlikeness in our everyday walking-around lives. The apostle Paul calls himself and us to imitate this fullness of reconciling all things: "For God in all his fullness was pleased to live in Christ, and through him God reconciled everything to himself. He made peace with everything in heaven and on earth by means of Christ's blood on the cross" (Col 1:19–20).

That said, Paul invites every follower of Jesus to live in this way, fully reconciling everything to him.

> Imitate me as I imitate Christ. (1 Cor 11:1)

> Imitate God, therefore, in everything you do. (Eph 5:1)

> Now these are the gifts Christ gave to the church: the apostles, the prophets, the evangelists, and the pastors and teachers. Their responsibility is to equip God's people to do his work and build up the church, the body of Christ. This will continue until we all come to such unity in our faith and knowledge of God's Son that we will be mature in the Lord, measuring up to the full and complete standard of Christ. (Eph 4:11–13)

> But whenever someone turns to the Lord, the veil is taken away. For the Lord is the Spirit, and wherever the Spirit of the Lord is, there is freedom. So all of us who have had that veil removed can see and reflect the glory of the Lord. And the Lord—who is the Spirit—makes us more and more like him as we are changed into his glorious image. (2 Cor 3:16–18)

To make this more practical and pointed for the minister, soul health, or in other words, spiritual formation, founded in the Gospels, history, and letters of the New Testament, is first for the minister. The New Testament is shot through with the embedded presence of leadership. Leadership is assumed to be present, from the Acts of the Apostles to the churches of Revelation. Therefore, recognizing the critical role of the identified minister in the context of church leadership is foundational. The Spirit seeks to leverage

---

6. Foster, *Streams of Living Water*, 21.

the increasingly holistic, balanced, and integrated soul health of the minister to provide an example for the church or to lead in the Way. Remember, a minister can't lead somewhere they don't live. How can a minister lead his members to drift the Jesus Way Reef if that minister hasn't learned to slow their soul, soften their focus, and have already drifted the reef themselves?

Please realize when I say, "leverage the increasingly holistic, balanced, integrated soul health of the minister," or "drift the Jesus Way Reef," I don't have in mind that you or I have it all together and live the Christ-life perfectly. As a leader on the path of soul health, I'm typically only a few steps ahead of those I lead. Perhaps Paul felt the same. However, as ministers, we are leading, so we must be ahead of those we lead, as we follow Christ.

To apply the snorkeling illustration here, after Brother Lee led me in the better way of passing over the reef, I went and led others to do the same. Leaders lead to where they live, to where they've been, and to see what they have seen. Not pointing into general spiritual mist and saying, "Good luck finding something." It's the opposite. Each Sunday morning, we emerge from the fog and say, "Follow me, I want to take you to where I've been, so you can know what I know, and see what I've seen. I know the way, follow me as I follow Christ." This kind of living as leading is an incarnational ministry.

Much like Jesus' incarnation was the visible image of the invisible God (Col 1:15), and Paul embodied the ongoing incarnation of Jesus (Gal 2:20) as an example for his church, we also follow Paul seeking to live in the kingdom of God like Jesus lived as an example for our flock to follow.

This lifestyle of leading and following flowed from the disciples to the early church leaders as they sought to flesh out this ongoing incarnational living in everyday life. In the early church season, the stark contrast between the kingdom of the world and God often meant life or death. Martyrdom for Christians was the default punishment for first, second, and third-century Roman leaders as applied to those who followed Christ with their whole lives, bowing to no king but King Jesus.

However, the end of this pervasive persecution occurred in the early fourth century with Emperor Diocletian. This abatement of persecution gave way to Constantine's Edict of Milan in AD 313, which released Christians from the perpetual "fight or flight" cultural context in which they were living. Therefore, by the end of the fourth century, life as a Christian had become quickly popular, comfortable, and eventually the only authorized

The Wrap-Up of Ministerial Soul Health

religion.[1] However, success can have its unintended consequences, leading to other forms of insidious bondage.[2]

In the fourth and fifth centuries, Christians who wanted to follow Jesus with all their heart, mind, and body were finding it increasingly difficult in the now comfortable and popular new religious climate. Deeply concerned with this impossible and increasing tension between following Jesus with radical conviction or with relaxed comfort, some, such as Antony, Pachomius, Macarius, Evagrius, and John Cassian, found no other way to resolve the tension than to flee to the desert as if driven by the Spirit as Christ was for the sake of being sanctified.[3]

Furthermore, Benedict famously built on Pachomius's original "rule" to offer a soul scaffolding of sorts. Benedict of Nursia's rule for healthy Christian living, whether in or out of the monastery, can be summarized as the rhythmic balancing of prayer and work.[4] Sounds a lot like work-life balance. I would add the element of play to his rule. So, pray, work, play, repeat. Not bad advice for contemporary Christians.

These early passionate men and women, and many who came after them, albeit peculiar, are examples of Christians seeking a complete set of soul gears, or people who craved a context for sold-out flourishing in the way of Jesus. A cursory survey of monastic biographies reveals extremes of charismatic and contemplative characteristics, with everything in between.

In one sense, monastics are often linked with the contemplative, and for good reason. These hyper-focused disciples of Christ pursued radical forms of commonly recognized contemplative practices such as silence, solitude, meditation, study, and fasting. Yet, on the other hand, they were also engaged in expressions of charismata, such as ecstatic visions or paralysis (slain in the Spirit?), words of knowledge, and often fantastical spiritual warfare.[5] One such example was Evagrius, who was blessed with the spiritual gift of discernment, resulting in being recognized with an unusual capacity to wisely speak into the lives of Christians seeking wisdom from the Spirit of God. This extraordinary gift of wisdom is much like some charismatics are today, with gifts such as words of knowledge and prophecy.[6]

1. Buxton, *Wisdom of the Desert*, 9.
2. Arndt, *Streams in the Wasteland*, 10.
3. Ward, *Desert Fathers*, loc. 139.
4. Benedict, *Rule of St. Benedict*, 78.
5. Ward, *Desert Fathers*, loc. 189.
6. Buxton, *Wisdom of the Desert*, 45.

Another sad conflation would be associating monastic life with extremes of emotionalism or legalistic performance-based faith. The bottom line from all the historical literature during this era of Christian history is that the vast majority of monks lived exclusively for loving union with God and others as the highest good. They wanted to make the great commandment as great as possible in their lives. In their cultural context, the desert was the best place for them to do that. Listen to evangelical pastor Andrew Arndt of New Life Church in Colorado Springs describe the general mindset of early monastics:

> This is what the Desert Fathers and Mothers—at their best—were after: the pure heart, the stripping away of everything in their lives that did not serve the purpose of love, the destruction of everything in their hearts that blocked or hindered the flow of the love of God in their lives. Love was what drew them to the desert. Love was the goal of their ongoing spiritual efforts. Everything they did was undertaken out of love for God and others. The point of spiritual discipline for them was the disciplining of the heart for this one thing: love.[7]

How about a word on what motivated early monastics from their mouth? John Cassian recorded many conferences he had with various desert fathers and mothers (by the way, "fathers and mothers" is simply a term of endearment and recognition of esteemed leadership in the monastic tradition); one of those conferences with a monastic leader named Moses had this to say about their motivation:

> Everything we do, our every objective, must be undertaken for the sake of this purity of heart. This is why we take on loneliness, fasting, vigils, work, and nakedness. For this, we must practice the reading of the Scripture, together with all the other virtuous activities, and we do so to trap and to hold our hearts free of the harm of every dangerous passion and in order to rise step by step to the high point of love.[8]

Could you write that about your devotional life today? I couldn't. They were so serious about sanctification. Overachievers.

My point in tracing back to the origins of soul health in the spiritual formation tradition is to demonstrate that, in the early days of the church, interest in denominational preeminence or earning salvation was of little to

---

7. Arndt, *Streams in the Wasteland*, 26–27.
8. Arndt, *Streams in the Wasteland*, 23.

no interest. The goal of the disciples, and those who soon followed behind them, such as the monastics, was to maximize Christlikeness in life, whatever the cost. Formal denominational arrogance had yet to arrive on the Christian history scene. Spiritual formation, therefore, as a movement, has its genesis in the gospel, not in a denomination.

In this cultural moment of the twenty-first century, I sense a return to passion for union with Christ, whatever the cost, beyond any union to a particular Christian denomination. A transdenominational movement, so to speak, that resists uniformity for unity with Christ, and ultimately with each other under the umbrella of Christianity. Protestant evangelicals are increasingly embracing contemplative characteristics and practices in the pursuit of loving union with Christ.[9]

Equally, in Catholic circles, both locally and nationally, a passionate embrace of Pentecostal worship elements is becoming increasingly evident. Perhaps, seeded by the often clandestine Charismatic Catholic Renewal movement in the 1970s, contemporary Catholics are openly and passionately engaging charismatic gears, as seen in the recent National Eucharistic Conference.[10]

From Christian leaders such as N. T. Wright to John Mark Comer, Christians of high and low church affiliations are integrating the best of all Christian traditions. Consider N. T. Wright, who openly reflected during an interview on the personal practice of speaking in tongues also endorsed it as contemplative prayer.[11] And how about John Mark Comer interviewing Strahan Coleman in the *Rule of Life* podcast, promoting the practice of staying in a room for hours and praying in tongues?[12]

The walls are coming down between Christian denominations. Many who are living out the way of Jesus in this cultural moment are so passionate about radically following Jesus into Christlikeness that they are integrating more and more of the best Christian orthodox practices from all the great faith traditions. Indeed, there is plenty of love and allegiance to faith traditions in this cultural moment, but the arrogance of faith silos is fading. This humbling in the body of Christ is a good thing.

9. Staton, "Contemplative Charismatic Ministry," is one such conversation.
10. "Revival Session," National Eucharistic Conference; when you visit the link, slide to various parts of the experience to see the integration of both charismatic and contemplative gears.
11. Wright, "Cessationism."
12. Comer, "Luminary Interview: Strahan Coleman."

No doubt blending the best of Christian faith traditions as a mosaic is a tricky endeavor. The word I just used is key, "orthodoxy." I'm not advocating for an "anything goes" openness. Not at all. I'm advocating for an openness to borrow the best practices from all Christian faith traditions, which, when integrated into an orthodox, compassionate, and morally convictional life, will result in robust Christlike living. Of course, there may be essential elements of orthodoxy that we may divide over for good reason. However, in this cultural moment, loving union with God and with one another is the only coherent witness to the Christian gospel. Holding denominational discernment in tension is real, but worth it for the sake of soul health and a coherent evangelistic gospel witness.

Imagine Catholics embracing more and more expository Bible preaching or Pentecostals practicing silence in their worship services. Imagine Baptists open to speaking in tongues as a biblical and practical form of prayer. Wow, we could keep our allegiance to tradition while advancing in transformation by borrowing best practices from each other. This balance of diversity and unity, in the context of convictional Christian orthodox doctrine, is evidenced by a passionate, Spirit-empowered life, and represents the current potential for Christian spiritual formation in this cultural moment.

Today's spiritual formation/soul health revival is anchored in this same tension between living in or of the world, as exemplified by the monastics. The struggle is real, and their struggle is our struggle. How do we live and lead toward holistic soul health in our cultural moment?

We lead toward soul health by beginning with ourselves. Soul health is foremost an individual and inward journey, seeking first personal healing from the soul disease of sinfulness through the saving and sanctifying work of Christ, and then applying that sanctifying cure of the Spirit to ourselves as we offer it to the people we lead as soul shepherds.

Again, for more on developing a fully geared soul transmission, check out *The Charismatic Contemplative Podcast* in appendix 1 or Lee University Preaching Center's YouTube channel.[13]

I took time to get into the Christian spiritual formation weeds because soul health demands an openness to the unfamiliar. Consider the following exercise of the nine-dot puzzle.

---

13. http://www.youtube.com/@LeeUniversityPreachingCenter.

THE WRAP-UP OF MINISTERIAL SOUL HEALTH

Draw four lines through all nine dots without lifting your pen. Lines can cross.

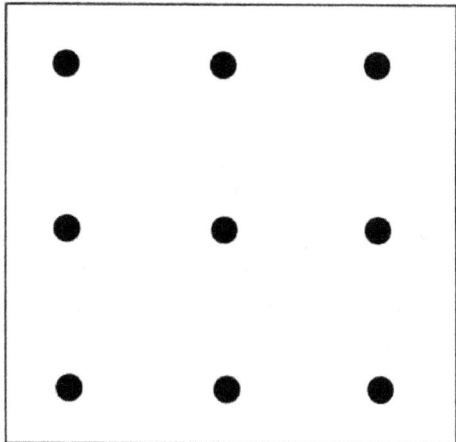

Thinking outside your box is the only way to grow beyond where you are now. Don't for a moment imagine that thinking outside the box of your current Christian faith tradition is somehow outside God's box of an orthodox, morally convictional frame. Consider the edges of this book's page as God's box. Now you can see that God's box is bigger than your box. Soul health requires a willingness to engage the unfamiliar but not the unorthodox. So, where silence and solitude may be unfamiliar to you, it's not unorthodox regarding Christian doctrine. Where speaking in tongues, raising your hands in worship, or dancing in the Spirit may be unfamiliar to you, these practices are not a betrayal of orthodox Christian faith or your tradition, but an enhancement as long as they are done in order and under your ministerial leadership's authority.

My wife was raised in a deep and vibrant Pentecostal context. She often talks about the angst she feels when engaging in contemplative practices. To her, at some level, contemplative spiritual disciplines like silence feel like a betrayal of her Pentecostal fidelity. When I listen to her talk this way, it gives me the impression that she interprets silence and solitude or meditation as somehow Christian faith tradition adultery.

As a non-charismatic, you may be reading this from the other end of the Christian faith spectrum and experience worshiping outside your faith tradition box in the reverse direction as my wife does. Imagine a Baptist clapping, dancing, or raising their hands. This worship expression may feel like a faith tradition adultery to them. Regardless of the direction,

The Uniqueness and Danger of Ministry

from charismatic to contemplative or contemplative to charismatic, and anywhere in between, growing beyond where you are right now in soul health will require you to get beyond the edges of your current soul box. Or, tracking back to the snorkeling illustration, soul health will require you to slow down, soften your focus, and imagine that you just may have missed something.

The appendices of this book are invitations for you to venture outside your soul box. They offer an embrace of ancient practices designed to maximize the great commandment of love in your soul. The resources listed are also for your ongoing exploration of the gospel-anchored spiritual formation movement. What comes next may be the most potent and practical part of this book; don't miss it.

Yeah, me too. I'm more of an inside-the-box thinker than I thought. Here's the solution.

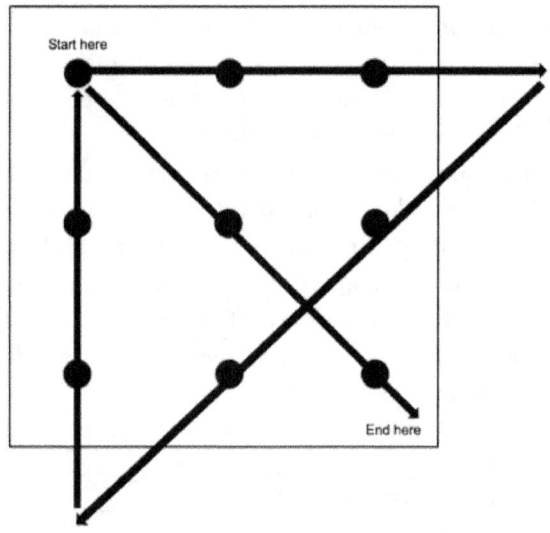

Epilogue

To complete the circle, I have written this book to say that this Buttercup doesn't have to suck it up. However, every buttercup minister must put in the effort to sustain their soul health and the soul health of their family in the most unique and dangerous vocational context.

Indeed, ministry is the most important vocation on the face of the planet. Being a minister is the most important job on the face of the planet. Preaching is the most important public speaking on the face of the planet. So, please take seriously your soul health and the soul health of your family. You and your church are God's gift to the world. He loved the world so much that he sent his only Son to die so that his church could be born, and you would be called to be a leader in it. The King of kings has called you out of standard Christian service to professional Christian service for such a time as this.

LaDon and I never for one second imagined you were intentionally neglecting your soul or the souls in your family. We just know how easy it is in professional ministry to be captivated by the divine calling and work. The immersive and eternal weight of ministry can insidiously lead you to attend to everyone else and neglect yourself and those closest to you. Don't let the devil fool you; embrace the warnings herein, and engage the fundamental practices of soul health offered.

Be sure the devil is prowling, seeking in particular a minister he can devour by perpetual distraction from their soul health. Fellow minister,

> We are not fighting against flesh-and-blood enemies, but against evil rulers and authorities of the unseen world, against mighty powers in this dark world, and against evil spirits in the heavenly places. Therefore, put on every piece of God's armor so you will be

The Uniqueness and Danger of Ministry

able to resist the enemy in the time of evil. Then after the battle, you will still be standing firm." (Eph 6:12–13)

WE>me!

We're in this together. We love you and your family.[1]

Steve and LaDon

---

1. If you would like more information on soul health clinics for leaders or churches, please visit www.ministryoasis.com.

Appendix 1

Resources

LaDon and I have curated a site for nurturing soul health in the minister and their family (www.ministryoasis.com) and *The Charismatic Contemplative Podcast* on YouTube.

Soul health videos by Steve: https://vimeo.com/user/99688025/folder/19293258

Soul health clinics for churches: https://vimeo.com/764653604

Appendix 1

Soul health clinics for ministers: https://vimeo.com/770048796

If by reading this book you've recognized that you're currently in an acute crisis of well-being, please reach out to the following for partnership:

- https://www.centerforministerialcare.com
- Vining Christian Counseling: johnkvining@gmail.com
- Via Counseling: https://www.viacounselingresources.com
- Family Christian Counseling: https://www.myfccc.com
- Christian Care Connection: https://christiancareconnect.com
- SafeHarbor Christian Counseling: https://www.safeharbor1.com

If by reading this book you've recognized that adding formal soul health experiences would be good for you, check out the following:

- The Pastor's Refuge: https://thepastorsrefuge.com
- The Resting Place Ministry: http://www.therestingplaceministry.org
- Selah Leaders: https://selahleaders.com
- Rplnish: https://www.rplnish.org

If by reading this book you've recognized an interest in furthering your understanding of spiritual formation/soul health, check out the following:

DIGITAL

- The best introduction to spiritual formation there is, John Mark Comer: https://www.practicingtheway.org
- Originating in the heart of Richard Foster and Dallas Willard, Renovaré: https://renovare.org
- The deepest collection of spiritual formation videos curated by Dr. Gary Moon: https://www.youtube.com/@conversatiodiv

PRINT

- Paul David Tripp: *Dangerous Calling*

Resources

- Dallas Willard: *Renovation of the Heart*
- John Ortberg: *Soul Care*
- Richard Foster: *Celebration of Discipline* and *Streams of Living Water*
- Rich Villodas: *The Deeply Formed Life*
- Ken Shigematsu: *God in My Everything*
- Lance Bacon: *Restore Such a One*
- Henri Nouwen: *The Way of the Heart*
- Diane Chandler: *Christian Spiritual Formation*
- James K. A. Smith: *You Are What You Love*
- Tyler Staton: *Praying Like Monks, Living Like Fools*

Appendix 2

Soul Health Planning (SHP) Toolkit

SHP WORKSHEET

Year:_____

Soul Goal

Take time to sit quietly in prayer with the Holy Spirit to collaborate on a statement regarding the big broad goal of this Soul Health Plan. . . . Be specific and clear. . . . No wrong answers.

Soul Word

Ask the Holy Spirit to give you one word that you could anchor your plan goal in—a word you could use as a breath prayer in meditation often.

Soul Health Planning (SHP) Toolkit

Soul Exercises

These may involve all or just one of the following time-sensitive modes.... Suggestions follow below.

Daily:

Weekly: *(Make sure you include a Sabbath)*

Monthly:

Annually:

Personal Practices

These are different than the exercises and explained in detail in the following pages. They may involve all or just one of the following time-sensitive modes.

Daily:

Weekly:

Monthly:

Annually:

Example 1

Soul Goal

To cultivate a non-anxious, unselfconscious presence where people feel refreshed in my presence as I only look to God for my metric of success, secure in his love alone.

Appendix 2

Soul Word

Safe. Because I am God's beloved, I am perfectly safe in God's universe.

Soul Exercises

>   **Daily**: Prayer of awaken and examen (see below for explanation), breathe soul word in prayer all day
>
>   **Weekly**: Sabbath Thursday sundown until Friday sundown, increase biblical and classic prayer memorization (ex. Lord's Prayer, Glory Be, Valley of Vision, etc.)
>
>   **Monthly**: Silence (see below for explanation)
>
>   **Annually**: Attend a guided retreat

Personal Practices

>   **Daily**: Ruthlessly eradicate all negative, cynical, deceptive, draining people, thought patterns, behaviors, and circumstances from my life; give someone my undivided attention and be very generous with affirmation; tell someone directly and emphatically I love them every day
>
>   **Monthly**: Directly challenge someone who is negative, cynical, deceptive, or draining to repent; be more courageous in my exhortation
>
>   **Annually**: Visit the National Museum of Art for a day of reflection

Example 2

Soul Goal

To live an increasingly open life to God, self, and others.

Soul Word:

Openness. Openness, as I understand it from the Holy Spirit, is to nurture a holistically open sense of life. I become available to changing circumstances by flowing adaptively with a welcoming attitude, adjusting with peace and trust in God. I have confidence in that, because I love God with all my heart, mind, and body, I am the safest person in the universe. Furthermore, I am living open to new people and experiences enthusiastically.

Soul Exercises

Daily: Prayer of awaken by breathing the "Our Father" and Ps 23. Prayer of examen by breathing a Ps 4:8, "In peace I will lie down and sleep, for you alone, O Lord, will keep me safe."

Weekly: Practice Sabbath in a more intentional way from sundown Thursday to sundown Friday (maybe use of a candle or do better at scheduling Sabbath experiences earlier)

Monthly: Fast a full day per month to make sure nothing captures my imagination and affection more than God

Personal Practices

Daily: Become increasingly more interested in new experiences and people; become hypervigilant to opportunities for openness

Bi-Monthly: Secure counseling for unresolved issues

Quarterly: Get away for two full days for rest and fun with LaDon

Annually: Spend time on a guided retreat

For more info related to SHPs: https://www.ministryoasis.com/resources.

Soul Health Plan (SHP) Explication and Exercise Catalog[1]

The SHP is meant to be easily accessible to anyone at any stage of their Christian experience. It is not intended to serve as a classic Rule of Life (*regula*

---

1. For a video explanation of why we need an SHP, see: www.youtube.com/watch?v=y4pCkDYopnA.

vitae) in the spiritual formation tradition. Instead, it is designed to serve as an introduction to the more comprehensive traditional Rule of Life.

Like you would make a plan for anything, just make a plan using the worksheet above to plan for your soul health. If you fail to plan for your soul, you plan to fail your soul. Make a plan today!

Sabbath

Rest is rooted in the creation story and the Decalogue (fourth commandment, Deut 5:12–15). Rest is holy to the Lord. Sabbath is not a day off or vacation; it is holy and to be a unique day in our week. The following Ss will help you keep this special day holy, a sanctuary in time.

- The Ss of sacred Sabbath:
    - *Supply*—in advance, supply the Sabbath with everything you need to make it rich. Secure food, tickets, gas, plans, etc., so you're free to rest. Get time-sensitive work done to supply margin to relax without worry.
    - *Stop*—cease all regular paid and unpaid work.
    - *Settle*—after the hard stop of work, front-load your Sabbath with exercises that give permission to settle all insecurities about work and trust God to have your back while you disconnect from work.
    - *Savor*—soak in only beauty, joy, peace, love, and fun; really savor the good. Only engage in activities that are restorative to your body and soul.
    - *Synchronize*—recognize that seeking to gain the world will distance your soul from God, the giver of life. Repent and synchronize your heart with God's love for you, his sovereignty, and providence.

Visit https://www.ministryoasis.com/resources for more resources on Sabbath.

Personal Practices

Personal practices are different than soul exercises in that they are tailored to you and your life which will not likely resonate with anyone else. They are specific actions that you establish at the direction of the Spirit for specific reasons in your current life stage and/or personality. For instance, imagine your father never said "I love you" to you and the Spirit brought this to your attention and the potential implications it has had. Perhaps this resulted in you not saying "I love you" to him or others. Therefore, a personal practice born of reflection in the Spirit may be to say "I love you" to all whom the Lord directs you to. Another possible personal practice could be to try new things, like Thai food, gardening, dancing, exercise, art, reading a book or blog by someone who disagrees with you, etc. The Spirit may identify a past trauma or offense you experienced and give you specific practices like counseling, grief work, letter writing, donating money, etc. related to the trauma or offense. There are no rules for personal practices, except that you open yourself to having some.

Dallas Willard established a Spirit-led personal practice one year: to never have the last word, letting the other have the last word.[2] This is very personal and unique to the individual.

Prayer of Awaken and Examen

The prayers of awaken and examen are ancient ways to bookend your day. It will take some conditioning to develop the soul habit of awakening to the Lord's presence and then examining your day in the Lord's presence each night. I recommend you simply use, for the morning awaken, Ps 19:14, "Lord, may the words of my mouth and the meditations of my heart be acceptable in Thy sight, my Lord and my redeemer."[3] Then for the evening examen, alter the verse slightly: "Lord, have the words of my mouth today and the meditations of my heart been acceptable in your sight?" Then reflect on your day in the Spirit.

Contemporary Soul Exercises

- *Media fast*: Deny ourselves all or some media to spend that attention on God's presence.
- *Praying for the success of our competitors*: Sit in God's presence and invite the Holy Spirit to show you who your competitors are. Be open to hearing what you don't want to hear.

2. Willard, *Living in Christ's Presence*, loc. 42.
3. My paraphrase of Ps 19:14.

Appendix 2

- *A day without guile*: Attempt to live one whole day not angling every situation or conversation for your benefit.
- *A day without talking negatively about others*: Only speak about others in positive language. Don't even report information that could be interpreted negatively.
- *An afternoon of silence at an art gallery or in nature.*
- *Sleep*: Commit to getting at least eight hours of sleep per night.
- *Practice hospitality*: Invite people to your home that you would not usually think of inviting into your home and treat them very well.
- *Play*: Commit to playing a game once per week with no other agenda than having fun. Forget winning as a goal.
- *Practice loving those we disagree with*: Intentionally spend time with people you don't agree with and treat them with grace, preferring to listen to them with no judgment and only love.

The following are creative, real-life personal practices that were reported to me from an everyday Christian friend. These street-level ideas will challenge your soul as new exercises at the gym would challenge your body. So, pick one or more and personalize them for yourself. Have at it![4]

- Fasting—No mints. I was addicted to wintergreen mints—eating thirty to thirty-five a day easily. Constantly throughout the day, I wanted to eat mints. It took prayer to get through.
- I needed to renew my mind. I stopped watching the news. I realized my mind was getting filled with useless stuff and causing me to think negatively (Rom 12:2).
- No radio. I drove in silence. I practiced praying and talking to the Lord while driving.
- "Never stop praying" 1 Thess 5:17.
- I woke up every morning and said, "Holy, holy, holy is the Lord God Almighty who was and is to come," before starting my day (Rev 4:8). This helped me start my day off by talking to the Lord.

---

4. I want to express my gratitude for a best friend like Roger McCracken. He is a model student of Soul Health as he absorbed the content I taught and modeled then offered his creative application tactics to challenge his soul.

Soul Health Planning (SHP) Toolkit

- Clean up my speech—I speak a lot of slang. So, I decided to clean it up and start saying "good morning" instead of "hey, what's up?" This was a tough one, but I thought it was important for people to take me seriously.
- No sarcastic remarks—First day, first hour, I realized I would have typically made about twelve smart comments! By being sarcastic, I wasn't encouraging the folks I was speaking to (Eph 4:29). Also, sarcasm tends to annoy folks, not bless them.
- Stop recreational cussing—No cuss words, even joking around. Clean up what comes out of my mouth (Eph 4:29).
- Listen more and speak less—Intentionally listen to people and not interrupt them (Prov 21:23). I realized I talked more than listened, and often I would make a mistake as a result. Therefore, I began listening more and thinking before speaking or reacting.
- No complaining (Phil 2:14)—By working on not being sarcastic and listening before speaking, I realized I complain a lot. So, I made it a point not to complain. My spouse noticed right away and quickly realized it was something I was working on.
- Read a book to help spiritual disciplines/prayer—I ended up reading several. They go hand in hand with Scripture reading.
- Start a reading group—I read the book *The Resolution for Men*. I got five guys to do it with me. We all signed resolutions.
- Live Rom 12—My spouse and I spent the whole month practicing Rom 12: being kind, not like the world, serve well, give generously, love others, work hard, etc.
- Memorize Scripture—Romans 8; I got about ten others involved to do it as well.
- Read the Bible daily—Invite someone to read with you for accountability.
- Make kind, unwarranted gestures to others—Go over and above to do things for them (Eph 5:28).
- Take moments of silence—Take intentional quiet breaks throughout the day to refocus and reset (Ps 46:10). This helps my mind refresh. I speak with God, breathe, and relax.

- Pray for work/school—My spouse/friend and I even went to my office/school every Sunday after church to pray over the building and everyone that worked there (Luke 11:9).
- No video gaming Monday through Friday—Gaming occupied too much of my time, taking time from God and others.
- Use a prayer list—I prayed daily but began using an actual prayer list.
- Invite at least one (unchurched) person to church each week—It was harder than it sounds, but it helped me learn to be open and look for opportunities to speak about church and God.
- Practice being in two places at once—Be at work and with Jesus at the same time; I was speaking with someone and with Jesus, etc. Everything I was doing, I just imagined Jesus was there. It changed how I spoke and how I conducted myself—Brother Lawrence-like.

Classic Soul Exercises[5]

Inward Exercises

Meditation—intentional focus of our attention on a particular attribute of God or passage of Scripture in order to crowd out the world and be alone with God.

- Exod 24:15-18
- Exod 33:11
- Exod 20:18–19
- Ps 1:1–3
- 1 Kgs 19:9–18
- Acts 10:9–20
- 2 Cor 12:1–4

Prayer—God's chosen method of access into his presence, where we encounter him relationally and are comforted, directed, and strengthened.

- Matt 6:5–15

---

5. These exercises are based on from Richard Foster's *Celebration of Discipline: The Path to Spiritual Growth*, found on page 235 of the Kindle edition.

Soul Health Planning (SHP) Toolkit

- Ps 103
- Ps 51
- Ps 150
- Matt 26:36–46
- Jas 5:13–18
- Mark 9:14–29

Fasting—intentionally denying and or controlling physical needs or desires to increase spiritual strength and sensitivity.

- Luke 4:1–13
- Isa 58:1–7
- Dan 10:1–14
- Neh 1:4–11
- Esth 4:12–17
- Acts 13:1–3
- Acts 14:19–23

Study—a means of knowing God by studiously learning his truths and identifying his priorities through the in-depth study of Scripture. This means dedicating an extended period of time (several hours) to the study of Scripture with the assistance of commentaries, concordances, and lexical aids.

- Prov 1:1–9; 23:12, 23
- Jas 1:5; Heb 4:11–13; 2 Tim 3:16–17
- Phil 4:8–9; Col 3:1–17
- Luke 10:38–42
- Ezra 7:10; Jas 1:19–25
- Acts 17:1–3, 10–12; 19:8–10
- Prov 24:30–34

APPENDIX 2

Outward Exercises

Simplicity—intentionally developing habits of living designed to produce freedom from worldly values regarding material things. It is practicing contentment with what we have by simplifying our life.

- Matt 6:19–24
- Matt 6:25–34
- Gen 15
- Lev 25:8–12
- Matt 5:33–37; Jas 5:12
- Amos 5:11–15, 24; Luke 4:16–21
- Luke 12:13–34

Silence and solitude—solitude is the intentional act of withdrawing from the presence of others to be in the presence of God in an undistracted way. Adding silence to solitude conditions oneself to listen for God's voice in an expectant and positive manner. This combination discipline is intended to discern direction from the Holy Spirit specifically or in general.

- Jas 3:1–12; Luke 23:6–9
- Matthew 6:5–6; Luke 5:16
- Ps 8
- Jer 20:7–18
- Matt 26:36–46
- Matthew 27:32–50
- Matthew 9:35–38, 23:37

Submission—the deliberate act of placing oneself under the authority of another as an act of obedience and humility.

- Mark 8:34; John 12:24–26
- Phil 2:1–11
- Gen 22:1–19
- Gal 2:19–21
- Matt 5:38–48

Soul Health Planning (SHP) Toolkit

- Eph 5:21–6:9, 1 Pet 3:1–9
- Rom 13:1–10; Acts 4:13–20, 5:27–29, 16:35–39

Service—involves doing things one would not normally do in the service of others rather than serving oneself.

- Matt 20:20–28
- John 13:1–17
- Exod 21:2, 5–6; 1 Cor 9:19
- Col 3:23–25
- Rom 12: 9–13
- Matt 25:31–39
- Luke 10:29–37

Corporate Exercises

Confession—the ritual practice of leaving your burdens at the foot of the cross. It is deliberately telling a trusted friend or advisor your deepest fears or greatest failures in confidence.

- Isa 59:1–9; Rom 3:10–18
- Jer 31:34; Matt 26:28; Eph 1:7
- 1 John 1:5–10
- 2 Tim 1:8–10; 1 Tim 2:5; 1 John 2:1
- Luke 15:11–24
- Matt 16:19, 18:18; John 20:23
- Jas 5:13–16

Worship—begins with proper knowledge of God and a dependent relational experience with him. It is proclaiming through our spirit an agreement with the Holy Spirit that the loving greatness of God holds us spellbound in awe and wonder of God's greatness.

- John 4:19–24
- John 6:52–58, 63

- Eph 5:18–20; Col 3:16–17
- Isa 6:1–8
- Ps 96
- Ps 148
- Rev 5:6–14

Guidance—takes place on different levels and through various agencies, such as Scripture, reason, circumstances, friends, pastors, coaches, and mentors, all of which are filtered through spiritual discernment as promptings of the Spirit.

- Heb 11
- Gen 24: 1–21
- Isa 1:17, 18–20
- Prov 3:5–6; John 14:6, 16:13; Acts 10:1–35
- Acts 16:6–10; 2 Corinthians 2:12
- Acts 21:8–14
- Rom 8:14, 28–30

Celebration—intentional choice to find God everywhere and in everything with joy and gladness.

- Exod 15:1–2, 20–21
- 2 Sam 6:12–19
- Ps 103
- Ps 150
- Luke 19:35–40; John 12:12–19
- Acts 3:1–10
- Rev 19:1–8

Soul Health Planning (SHP) Toolkit
General Soul Health Exercises

The Lord's Prayer in your own words:

Our Father in heaven, hallowed be your name.

Your kingdom come, your will be done, on earth as it is in heaven.

Give us this day our daily bread,

and forgive our sinfulness as we forgive those who sin against us.

Don't let us yield to temptation, but rescue us from the evil one.

For yours is the kingdom, the power and the glory.

Amen!

Appendix 2

The Lord's Prayer in your own words (example):

Our Father in heaven, hallowed by your name.
Dear Dad, you are the most cherished person in my life.
Your kingdom come, your will be done, on earth as it is in heaven.
I want to imitate you as your dearly loved child. I want my life to look like yours.
Give us this day our daily bread,
I'm convinced you are my life sustenance each day, trusting that I have all I need because you are my Shepherd.
and forgive our sinfulness as we forgive those who sin against us.
Forgive me for not living like you, and help me forgive those whose not living like you impacts me.
Don't let us yield to temptation, but rescue us from the evil one.
Please help me detect the schemes of the world, the flesh, and the devil, and show me the clear way around or out of their traps, giving me the courage to do what it takes to seek first your kingdom.
For yours is the kingdom, the power and the glory.
I declare that you have all the power in my life as I live in your kingdom with you as my king forever.
Amen!
May it be so!

Soul Health Planning (SHP) Toolkit

Psalm 23 in your own words:

(Follow the pattern above of The Lord's Prayer in your own words.)

The Lord is my shepherd; I have all that I need.

He lets me rest in green meadows; he leads me beside peaceful streams.

He renews my strength. He guides me along right paths, bringing honor to his name.

Even when I walk through the darkest valley, I will not be afraid, for you are close beside me.

Your rod and your staff protect and comfort me.

You prepare a feast for me in the presence of my enemies.

You honor me by anointing my head with oil. My cup overflows with blessings.

Surely your goodness and unfailing love will pursue me all the days of my life, and I will live in the house of the Lord forever.

Bibliography

Alloy, Lauren B., et al. *Abnormal Psychology: Current Perspectives*. New York: McGraw-Hill, 1996.

American Psychiatric Association. *Diagnostic and Statistical Manual of Mental Disorders, 4th ed., Text Revision*. Washington, DC: American Psychiatric Association, 2000.

Arndt, Andrew. *Streams in the Wasteland: Finding Spiritual Renewal with the Desert Fathers and Mothers*. Colorado Springs: NavPress, 2022. Kindle ed.

Bacon, Lance M. *Restore Such a One: Holistic Restoration for Ministers, Families, and Churches Following a Sexual Moral Failure*. Eugene, OR: Wipf & Stock, 2024. Kindle ed.

Baker, D. C., and J. P. Scott. "Predictors of Well-Being Among Pastors' Wives: A Comparison with Non-Clergy Wives." *The Journal of Pastoral Care* 46.1 (1992) 33–43.

Barna Group. "Pastors Share Top Reasons They've Considered Quitting Ministry in the Last Year." Apr. 27, 2022. https://www.barna.com/research/pastors-quitting-ministry/.

―――. *The Relationships of Today's Pastors: 10 Insights on Marriage, Parenting and the Personal Connections Shaping Life in Ministry*. Barna Group, 2025.

Benedict. *The Rule of St. Benedict*. Translated by Boniface Verheyen. N.p.: Planet Monk Books, 2018.

Benuto, Lorraine T., et al. "Secondary Traumatic Stress Among Victim Advocates: Prevalence and Correlates." *Journal of Evidence-Informed Social Work* 15.5 (2018) 494–509.

Bloom, Matt. *Flourishing in Ministry: How to Cultivate Clergy Wellbeing*. London: Rowman & Littlefield, 2019.

Bowers, James P., ed. *Portrait and Prospect: Church of God Pastors Face the 21st Century*. Cleveland, TN: Pentecostal Theological Seminary, 2004.

Brueggemann, Walter. *Sabbath as Resistance: Saying No to the Culture of Now*. New edition with study guide. Louisville, KY: Presbyterian Corporation, 2017.

Bryan, Jennifer L., et al. "God, Can I Tell You Something? The Effect of Religious Coping on the Relationship Between Anxiety over Emotional Expression, Anxiety, and Depressive Symptoms." *Psychology of Religion and Spirituality* 8.1 (2016) 46–53.

Bulgakov, Sergei. *The Bride of the Lamb*. Translated by Boris Jakim. Grand Rapids: Eerdmans, 2002.

Bibliography

Buxton, Nicholas. *The Wisdom of the Desert with Nicholas Buxton: The Origins, Way of Life and Spiritual Practice of Christian Monasticism, the Spiritual Teachings of Evagrius.* N.p.: Wise Studies, 2020.

Chan, Simon. *Liturgical Theology.* Downers Grove, IL: InterVarsity, 2006.

Chand, Samuel. *Leadership Pain: The Classroom for Growth.* Nashville: Thomas Nelson, 2015.

Chandler, Diane J. *Christian Spiritual Formation: An Integrated Approach for Personal and Relational Wholeness.* Downers Grove, IL: InterVarsity, 2014.

Clarke, M. A., et al. "Role-Related Stress and Adversity Impacting Christian Clergy Resilience: A Pan-Canadian Study." *Journal of Pastoral Care & Counseling* 77.1 (2023) 51–63.

Comer, John Mark, "Luminary Interview: Strahan Coleman." *Rule of Life* (podcast), Feb. 20, 2023. https://podcasts.apple.com/us/podcast/rule-of-life/id1646299048?i=1000600517540.

———. *The Ruthless Elimination of Hurry: How to Stay Emotionally Healthy and Spiritually Alive in the Chaos of the Modern World.* New York: Random House, 2019.

Culbertson, Howard. "Resources: Christian Missions and World Evangelism." Southern Nazarene University, 2025. https://home.snu.edu/~hculbert/index.htm.

Daniel, Lillian. "The Pastor's Husband: Redefining Expectations." *The Christian Century* 126.14 (2009) 28–31.

Daniels, Marc, dir. *I Love Lucy.* Season 1, episode 1, "The Girls Want to Go to a Nightclub." CBS, 1951.

Del Giudice, Marco, et al. "Programmed to Learn? The Ontogeny of Mirror Neurons." *Developmental Science* 12.2 (2009) 350–63.

Drumm, Rene, et al. "'Love Everybody, Keep Your Mouth Shut, Don't Have an Opinion': Role Expectations Among Seventh-Day Adventist Pastor Spouses." *Social Work & Christianity* 44.3 (2017) 94–114.

Erickson, Millard J. *Christian Theology.* Grand Rapids: Baker, 1986.

Foster, Richard. *Celebration of Discipline: The Path to Spiritual Growth.* New York: HarperCollins, 1998.

———. *Prayer: Finding the Hearts True Home.* New York: HarperCollins, 1992.

———. "Salvation as a Life." Renovaré, Sept. 2004. https://renovare.org/articles/salvation-as-a-life.

———. *Streams of Living Water: Celebrating the Great Traditions of Christ.* New York: HarperCollins, 2001.

Frankl, Viktor E. *Man's Search for Meaning.* Boston: Beacon, 2006.

Friedman, Edwin H. *A Failure of Nerve: Leadership in the Age of the Quick Fix.* Revised ed. New York: Church, 2017.

Gardner, Benjamin, and Amanda L. Rebar. "Habit Formation and Behavior Change." *Oxford Research Encyclopedias* 9.1 (2019). https://doi.org/10.1093/acrefore/9780190236557.013.129.

Gardner, Benjamin, et al. "How Does Habit Form? Guidelines for Tracking Real-World Habit Formation." *Cogent Psychology* 9.1 (2022). https://doi.org/10.1080/23311908.2022.2041277.

Garland, David E. *The New American Commentary: 2 Corinthians.* Nashville: Broadman and Holman, 1999. Kindle ed.

Gerander, Jerome T. "Compassion Fatigue: A Problem for Pastors." *Logia* 20.4 (2021) 19–26.

Bibliography

Giang, Vivian. "What It Takes to Change Your Brain After Age 25." *Fast Company*, Apr. 28, 2015. https://www.fastcompany.com/3045424/what-it-takes-to-change-your-brains-patterns-after-age-25.

Gleadow, Ewan, "Boy Dylan's Perfect Four-Word Response to Being Heckled as 'Judas' on Stage." Irish Star, Mar. 4, 2025. https://www.irishstar.com/culture/music-nightlife/bob-dylans-perfect-four-word-34794906.

Hall, Travis. "The Quickest Way to Lose Yourself Is to Compare Yourself." *Transformational Truths with Pastor Travis Hall* (podcast), Oct. 25, 2022. https://creators.spotify.com/pod/profile/travis-hall42/.

Hanewinckel, Jessica. "Mike Burnette: It's Not About the Numbers." *Outreach Magazine*, Sept./Oct. 2021, 140–42.

Harvey, Glynnis. "What's Left: The Role of a Politician's Spouse." *The Colgate Maroon-News*, Feb. 14, 2019. https://thecolgatemaroonnews.com/1582/commentary/whats-left-the-role-of-a-politicians-spouse/.

Heschel, Abraham Joshua. *The Sabbath*. New York: Farrar, Straus and Giroux, 2005.

Keller, Jan, et al. "Habit Formation Following Routine-Based Versus Time-Based Cue Planning: A Randomized Controlled Trial." *British Journal of Health Psychology* 26.3 (2021) 807–24.

Milner, Peter. "A Brief History of the Hebbian Learning Rule." *Canadian Psychology / Psychologie canadienne* 44.1 (2003) 5–9.

Mulholland, Robert M. *Invitation to a Journey: A Road Map for Spiritual Formation*. Downers Grove, IL: InterVarsity, 2016.

Muller, Wayne. *Sabbath: Finding Rest, Renewal, and Delight in Our Busy Lives*. New York: Bantam, 1999.

Murphy-Geiss, Gail. *Clergy Spouses and Families in the United Methodist Church 2009 Part II: Local Church Expectations and What Clergy Spouses Most Want the UMC to Know*. Chicago: The General Commission on the Status and Role of Women, 2009.

Muse, Stephen, et al. "Intensive Out-Patient Therapy for Clergy Burnout: How Much Difference Can a Week Make?" *Journal of Religious Health* 55.1 (2016) 147–58.

Nesbitt, P. D. "Marriage, Parenthood, and the Ministry: Differential Effects of Marriage and Family on Male and Female Clergy Careers." *Sociology of Religion* 56.4 (1995) 397–415.

Newberg, Andrew, and Mark Robert Waldman. *How God Changes Your Brain: Breakthrough Findings from a Leading Neuroscientist*. New York: Random House, 2009.

Newbigin, Lesslie. *Foolishness to the Greeks: The Gospel of Western Culture*. Grand Rapids: Eerdmans, 1986.

Nouwen, Henri. *The Way of the Heart*. New York: HarperCollins, 1981.

Nystrom, David P. *James*. The NIV Application Commentary 16. Grand Rapids: Zondervan Academic, 1997. Kindle ed.

Oden, Thomas C. *Classic Christianity: A Systematic Theology*. New York: HarperCollins, 1992.

Ortberg, John. *Soul Keeping: Caring for the Most Important Part of You*. Grand Rapids: Zondervan, 2014.

Peterson, Eugene H. *A Long Obedience in the Same Direction: Discipleship in an Instant Society*. Downers Grove, IL: InterVarsity, 2000. Kindle ed.

———. *The Pastor: A Memoir*. New York: HarperCollins, 2011.

Piper, John. "'I Never Made a Sacrifice': The Call and Question of David Livingstone." *Desiring God*, Mar. 19, 2018. https://www.desiringgod.org/articles/i-never-made-a-sacrifice.

Portal, Pete. *How to Be (Un)Successful: An Unlikely Guide to Human Flourishing*. Woking, UK: 24-7 Prayer, 2023.

Reed, Angela. "Rooted in Relationship: Longevity in a Congregational Ministry." *Review and Expositor Journal* 113.3 (2016) 303–14.

"Revival Session." National Eucharistic Conference, July 19, 2024. https://www.youtube.com/watch?v=lEI4GEJmHeo&list=WL&index=30.

Root, Andrew. *The Pastor in a Secular Age*. Ada, MI: Baker, 2019.

Scazzero, Peter. *The Emotionally Healthy Leader: How Transforming Your Inner Life Will Deeply Transform Your Church, Team, and the World*. Grand Rapids: Zondervan, 2015.

Shyamalan, M. Night, dir. *The Village*. Burbank, CA: Touchstone, 2004.

Shelley, Marshall. *Well-Intentioned Dragons: Ministering to Problem People in the Church*. Waco, TX: Word, 1985.

Staton, Tyler. "Contemplative Charismatic Ministry." Practicing the Way Pastors Conference, Nov. 12, 2024. https://www.youtube.com/watch?v=95g1oyUIdTA.

Spurgeon, Charles H. "He That Can Toy with His Ministry and Count It to Be Like a Trade. . ." AZ Quotes. https://www.azquotes.com/quote/1062317#google_vignette.

Sword, Rosemary K. M., and Philip Zimbardo, "Hurry Sickness: Is the Quest to Do All and Be All Costing Us Our Health?" *Psychology Today* (blog), Feb. 9, 2013, https://www.psychologytoday.com/us/blog/the-time-cure/201302/hurry-sickness.

Thayer's Greek Lexicon, Electronic Database. 2011. Biblesoft, Inc. https://www.blueletterbible.org/lexicon/g225/kjv/tr/0-1/.

Thompson, Curt. *Anatomy of the Soul: Surprising Connections Between Neuroscience and Spiritual Practices That Can Transform Your Life and Relationships*. Carol Stream, IL: Tyndale House, 2010.

Tozer, A. W. *The Pursuit of God*. Annotated and Illustrated. Hilton Head Island, SC: Starbooks, 2014.

Tripp, Paul David. *Dangerous Calling: Confronting the Unique Challenges of Pastoral Ministry*. Wheaton, IL: Crossway, 2012.

Vesley, Franz J. "Alleged Quote." Viktor Frankl Institut. https://www.viktorfrankl.org/quote_stimulus.html.

Villodas, Rich. *The Deeply Formed Life: Five Transformative Values to Root Us in the Way of Jesus*. Colorado Springs: WaterBrook, 2020.

Visker, Joseph, et al. "Ministry-Related Burnout and Stress Coping Mechanisms Among Assemblies of God-Ordained Clergy in Minnesota." *Journal of Religion and Health* 56.3 (2017) 951–61.

Ward, Benedicta. *The Desert Fathers: Sayings of the Early Christian Monks*. New York: Penguin Classics, 2003.

Willard, Dallas. *The Great Omission: Reclaiming Jesus's Essential Teachings on Discipleship*. New York: HarperCollins, 2006. Kindle ed.

———. *Living in Christ's Presence: Final Words on Heaven and the Kingdom of God*. Lisle, IL: IVP Formatio, 2013. Kindle ed.

———. *Renovation of the Heart: Putting on the Character of Christ*. Colorado Springs: NavPress, 2002.

Bibliography

Wolff, Hans W. *Anthropology of the Old Testament*. Translated by Margaret Kohl. London: SCM, 1974.

Wright, N. T., and Justin Brierley. "Cessationism and Why I Pray in Tongues / Ask N. T. Wright Anything." Premier Unbelievable, May 31, 2020. https://www.youtube.com/watch?v=slaoT4X-I8o.

Zigarelli, Michael. "Distracted from God: A Five-Year, Worldwide Study." *Christianity 9 to 5*, July 30, 2007. www.christianity9to5.com/distracted-from-god.

www.ingramcontent.com/pod-product-compliance
Lightning Source LLC
Chambersburg PA
CBHW062046220426
43662CB00010B/1669